...shed ...ands, ...ravel.

For more than 135 years our guidebooks have unlocked the secrets of destinations around the world, sharing with travellers a wealth of experience and a passion for travel.

Rely on Thomas Cook as your travelling companion on your next trip and benefit from our unique heritage.

Thomas Cook **pocket** guides

EDINBURGH

Thomas Cook

Your travelling companion since 1873

Written and updated by Zoë Ross
Original photography by Robin Gauldie

Published by Thomas Cook Publishing
A division of Thomas Cook Tour Operations Limited
Company registration no. 3772199 England
The Thomas Cook Business Park, 9 Coningsby Road,
Peterborough PE3 8SB, United Kingdom
Email: books@thomascook.com, Tel: +44 (0) 1733 416477
www.thomascookpublishing.com

Produced by Cambridge Publishing Management Limited
Burr Elm Court, Main Street, Caldecote CB23 7NU
www.cambridgepm.co.uk

ISBN: 978-1-84848-410-8

CONTENTS

INTRODUCING EDINBURGH

MAKING THE MOST OF EDINBURGH

THE CITY OF EDINBURGH

OUT OF TOWN TRIPS

PRACTICAL INFORMATION

INDEX

MAPS

SYMBOLS KEY

The following symbols are used throughout this book:

address telephone website address opening times important

The following symbols are used on the maps:

information office
airport
hospital
police station
bus station
railway station
cathedral
numbers denote featured cafés & restaurants

point of interest
city
large town
small town
motorway
main road
minor road
railway

Hotels and restaurants are graded by approximate price as follows:

£ budget price ££ mid-range price £££ expensive

The Firth of Forth and the Lomond Hills beyond Edinburgh Castle

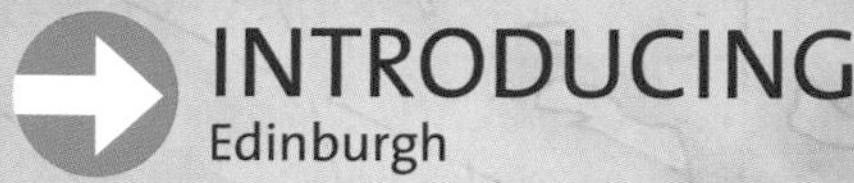

INTRODUCING
Edinburgh

Introduction

Perched on the prehistoric remains of a volcanic landscape and on the edge of the Forth flowing out to the North Sea, Edinburgh, nicknamed the 'Athens of the North', is considered by many to be Britain's most beautiful city.

Divided in two between the medieval Old Town and the 18th-century New Town, the city centre has a split personality. While you can soak up the romantic atmosphere of cobbled streets and tiny alleyways, and sense the power of the great Stewart monarchs in and around the Royal Mile, so too can you marvel at the vision and grandeur of the Georgian architects who created such splendid crescents and circuses for the privileged classes beneath the castle's gaze. Even if history isn't your thing, you can't fail to be impressed by the brooding spires, rugged crags and windswept coastline that all form part of Edinburgh's charm.

The Edinburgh Festival and the New Year's Hogmanay are the most popular times to visit, but don't miss the opportunity to come or return at other quieter times of year, when the world-class museums and exhibition centres can be taken in at a more leisurely pace. And don't overlook the superb shopping and dining possibilities. For a city that was once considered rather matronly, designer outlets and haute cuisine have entered Edinburgh's consciousness and have changed her face into a true style destination. Part of this turnaround has been due to the confidence boost Edinburgh received after the return of the Scottish Parliament to the city in 1999. For a decade or so prior to that it had clearly been playing second fiddle to its rival Glasgow in the tourist stakes. Meanwhile, the University of Edinburgh, considered one of the best places of learning in Britain, gives the city a youthful buzz for most of the year.

It's not all about urban attractions, either. One of the most attractive aspects of Edinburgh life is that within just a few kilometres you can be outside the city bustle and deep in the heart of rolling countryside, breathing in fresh Scottish air.

Historic Victoria Street winds up from the Grassmarket

When to go

Edinburgh is a great place to visit at any time of the year, as there is plenty to do and see, and most of its attractions are not weather-dependent.

SEASONS & CLIMATE

Edinburgh's climate rarely differs from that of the south by more than a few degrees in winter, and settled snowfall is usually reserved for the outer-city areas. That said, on windy days, the temperature can feel bitter, as the gusts sweep in off the coast, and hats, scarves and gloves are definitely called for. Temperatures between November and March average 3–12°C (37–53°F). Hot summers, however, are also a rarity, although fine, sunny days can add a wonderful glow to the city landscape. Summer temperatures average 15–23°C (59–73°F). Weather in Edinburgh is also changeable by the hour, so visitors should always be prepared. While winter lacks the warmth, there are plenty of things to attract visitors including the atmospheric Christmas Festival market on Princes Street Gardens (see page 13). In contrast, while summer may be a nicer climate in which to explore, crowds of tourists, particularly during the Edinburgh Festival (see page 14), can make the streets a challenge to navigate.

ANNUAL EVENTS

Edinburgh has a jam-packed calendar of annual events, as well as events that might be specific to a certain year. Carnivals, markets, sporting fixtures and street fairs all combine to make this one of the most party-happy cities in Britain. Listings magazines such as *The List* highlight any particular activities for that week of publication, and the tourist office (see page 151) will also have details of current and up-and-coming activities.

January

Burns Night (25 Jan) The Scottish poet Robert Burns is honoured throughout the city. Meals begin with the *Selkirk Grace*, in which the company claps while a piper leads the chef, carrying the haggis, to the top table. Next comes the recitation of Burns' famous poem *To a Haggis*. After the meal there are speeches, including the *Immortal Memory* speech dedicated to Burns' work and a *Toast to the Lassies*, ending with a rendition of *Auld Lang Syne*.

April

Ceilidh Culture (early April) A celebration of traditional Scottish songs, music, dance and storytelling held in locations throughout the city. Ⓦ www.ceilidhculture.co.uk

June

Pride Scotia (mid-June) Edinburgh's version of Gay Pride. There are events all around the city.

Royal Highland Show (late June) The agricultural show draws crowds with showjumping, sheep shearing and livestock displays. Ⓦ www.royalhighlandshow.org

July & August

Jazz & Blues Festival (late July–early Aug) A city-wide jazzfest that includes Jazz on a Summer's Day, a series of open-air concerts. Ⓦ www.edinburghjazzfestival.com

August

Edinburgh Mela (early Aug) Scotland's multicultural celebration in Pilrig Park, with a strong emphasis on Asia.

Expect bands, dances, Bollywood spectacles and much more. www.edinburgh-mela.co.uk

The Edinburgh Festival & Fringe The city surrenders itself to the world-renowned cultural festival (see page 14).

Edinburgh Military Tattoo An orgy of pageantry and pomp, held in front of the floodlit castle. The three-week event is so popular that it is broadcast on television all over the world and more than 200,000 people attend. The tattoo starts with Scottish regimental bands emerging, carrying effigies of William Wallace and Robert the

Marchers in the world-famous military tattoo in Edinburgh

Bruce and playing traditional Scottish songs. The finale is a rousing rendition of the *Evening Hymn*, the sounding of the *Last Post* and the *Lone Piper*, before a spectacular fireworks display. Tickets are hard to come by but go on sale in August for the following year.
ⓐ Tattoo Ticket Sales Office, 32–34 Market Street ⓣ (0131) 225 1188
ⓦ www.edintattoo.co.uk

Edinburgh International Book Festival (last half of Aug) Writers gather from all over the world to discuss their work.
ⓦ www.edbookfest.co.uk

Thousands celebrate Hogmanay in Edinburgh

Edinburgh International Film Festival (late Aug) Screenings of new releases, independent and art-house films, and talks and retrospectives of actors and directors. ⓐ Charlotte Square Gardens ⓦ www.edfilmfest.org.uk

December

The Edinburgh Christmas Festival Perhaps unexpectedly, this includes a traditional German market selling toys and trinkets, as well as live entertainment. ⓐ Princes Street Gardens

Hogmanay New Year's Celebrations Vast crowds of up to 100,000 people join the street party to watch fireworks and live bands. On 29 December there is a torchlight procession, on 30 December (known as 'The Night Afore') street performers do their stuff, and on New Year's Day the One O'Clock Run race takes place down the Royal Mile.

PUBLIC HOLIDAYS

New Year's Day 1 Jan
Day after New Year's Day 2 Jan
Good Friday 22 Apr 2011; 6 Apr 2012
Early May Bank Holiday first Monday in May
Spring Bank Holiday last Monday in May
Summer Bank Holiday first Monday in Aug
St Andrew's Day 30 Nov
Christmas Day 25 Dec
Boxing Day 26 Dec

If Christmas Day, Boxing Day, New Year's Day, 2 January or St Andrew's Day fall on a Saturday or Sunday, the next weekday becomes a public holiday.

The Edinburgh Festival & Fringe

For the month of August Edinburgh becomes unrecognisable from its normally sedate image, when the capital is overrun with actors, street buskers, musicians, dancers and a whole load of tourists who flock here to perform or watch a vast array of dramatic offerings.

Both the International Festival and the Fringe began in 1947. The International Festival is a professional performing arts festival offering a packed programme of theatre, dance and music in all the city's main theatres and many other venues too. Well-established theatre companies from all over the world come here to offer the capital their talents.

The Fringe was begun as a cultural post-war initiative to encourage those outside the mainstream of the performing arts to stage their own shows, and this continues to this day – anyone can perform at the Fringe as long as they book their venue well enough in advance. Today, performers come from all over the globe, aiming to achieve press attention and rave reviews for their work, and to be a part of the largest arts festival in the world. Over recent years more than 700 groups or individuals have performed here each year. One of the most popular parts of the Fringe is the comedy element, with stand-up comedians all vying for the prestigious if.comedy Award (formerly the Perrier Award), which has launched the careers of such titter merchants as Frank Skinner and Al Murray. Away from the indoor venues, the streets of the city are also full of celebratory verve. This is particularly true of the Royal Mile, which is crammed with buskers, mime artists and portrait painters for the month of the Festival.

The Festivals can be quite overwhelming. There's so much to see and do that it can be hard to choose, and the crowds make getting to venues and securing tickets quite a challenge. Each year a Festival

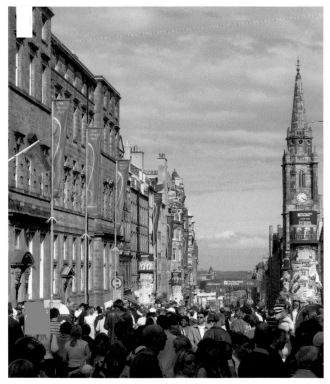

Festival-goers fill the streets of Edinburgh

programme is published, detailing what's on and where, and it pays to study it and decide what is of interest beforehand, not least because for the most popular events tickets sell out very fast indeed.

Fringe Box Office (0131) 226 0026 www.edinburghfestivals.co.uk

History

Edinburgh's hills – Arthur's Seat, Blackford Hill, Craiglockhart Hill and Castle Rock itself – are natural fortresses that attracted settlers as early as the first millennium BC. Castle Rock may even have been occupied for many centuries before the Roman invasion of Caledonia in AD 80–84. The Romans, however, bypassed Castle Rock but built a fort at Cramond, on the Firth of Forth.

In the 6th century AD, Castle Rock was a stronghold of the Christian British kingdom of the Gododdin, who called it Dun Eideann (Eideann's Fort), a name which became Edinburgh or 'Edwin's Fortress', after the Anglo-Saxon conquest of southeast Scotland in the 7th century AD. The Angles were eventually ousted by Malcolm II, King of Scots, in 1018 and Edinburgh and its castle soon grew in size and importance. In 1128, King David II founded Holyrood Abbey, at the foot of the Royal Mile. Over the following centuries Edinburgh grew to occupy the hillsides between Holyrood and the castle – the district now known as the Old Town.

Too close to the border for comfort, Edinburgh was frequently sacked and occupied by the English, and the city did not become Scotland's capital until 1436, when King James II (1430–60) made it his royal seat. Previous Scots kings had ruled from Dunfermline in Fife or Dumbarton on the Clyde, but Edinburgh was to be the home of the Scottish Crown and the Stewart dynasty for almost three centuries.

The Stewarts were unlucky monarchs – James II was killed when he was blown up by one of his own cannons, James III was assassinated by discontented nobles, James IV died in battle against the English at Flodden in 1513, James V died of despair after yet another defeat at English hands at Solway Moss, and his daughter

Mary was executed by her cousin Queen Elizabeth I of England. With the Union of the English and Scottish Crowns in 1603 her son, James VI of Scotland, became James I of England, ushering in a more peaceful era, although Edinburgh continued to change hands between Scottish, Royalist and Parliamentarian forces during the civil wars of the mid-17th century, when Scotland sided with King Charles I – another unlucky Stewart, beheaded in 1649.

The Act of Union of 1707, uniting Scotland with England, ended Edinburgh's glory days as Scotland's capital, although Bonnie Prince Charlie briefly made it his base in 1745. In other ways, however, the 18th century was a golden age for Edinburgh, which became a centre for philosophy, science and the arts.

With the Industrial Revolution, Edinburgh spread to include the seaport of Leith and new suburbs such as Portobello, while railways connected it with London and the rest of Britain. But the loss of political power to London and economic pre-eminence to Glasgow, Scotland's new industrial powerhouse, undermined some of Edinburgh's self-confidence.

The birth of the Edinburgh International Festival in 1947 (see page 14) was the start of a deliberate campaign to restore the city's fortunes, which culminated half a century later in devolution and the return of a Scottish Parliament to Edinburgh after 290 years of rule from London. Edinburgh entered the 21st century as the true capital of Scotland once again, and, in 2004, the opening of the new Scottish Parliament building in Holyrood (see page 72) underlined the city's political eminence. Despite the national coalition government between the Conservatives and the Liberal Democrats in spring 2010, Scotland has always been a Labour stronghold. However, it's the Scottish National Party that is currently in power in Scotland, under the leadership of First Minister Alex Salmond.

Lifestyle

The citizens of Edinburgh are generally considered to be rather reserved and taciturn, particularly in comparison to their more gregarious neighbours in Glasgow, although anyone who has experienced the unfriendly anonymity of many capital cities would find this quite absurd. In reality, hop into any taxi or queue up at any shop counter and you'll find the locals like nothing better than to pass the time of day, usually with some reference to the weather.

And it is the weather that largely shapes the capital's character. From wet to sunny to wet again in a matter of hours, the changeability means that although Edinburghers love to snuggle in warm pubs and exchange gossip over a pint of beer, they rarely miss an opportunity to get to the great outdoors when a hint of sunshine comes through.

Edinburgh may be a capital, but it's a small one. While property prices continue to rise, many locals are still able to afford to live in or very near the city centre. This makes for a communal, convivial atmosphere where work and home live side by side. There's also little of the age divide that dominates many city landscapes. While there are bars and clubs that are exclusively the preserve of the young, you're far more likely to see trendy university students sitting happily beside septuagenarians in the city's multitude of old-style pubs.

The face of the city changes entirely in August, however, when the world and his wife descend on Edinburgh for the annual arts festival. While locals are justifiably proud of the event, many see it as an opportunity to get away, not least for the extortionately high prices that they can charge for renting out their flats or homes at a time when accommodation is at a premium.

Clearly August is prime tourist season, but don't expect a cultural wasteland the rest of the time. Visitors flock here all the year round, and you'll hear as many accents from the rest of Britain and the world as you will the traditional Scottish brogue from people who have chosen to make this beautiful city their home.

A Scotsman in his kilt shoots (or rather catches) the breeze

Culture

Edinburgh is one of Britain's cultural hotspots with festivals, theatrical events, music and dance going on all year round. The information given here is a general overview of what you might expect, but to find out more about what is going on at the time of your visit head to the tourist office on Princes Street (see page 151) or any newsagent to pick up a copy of the city's listings magazine *The List* or visit the website ⓦ www.edinburgh.org

Edinburgh's theatrical highlight is undoubtedly the Festival (see page 14) but the rest of the year is also a hotbed of activity, presenting both Scottish-based events as well as national and international touring companies. While most of the national companies, including Scottish Ballet, Opera and Orchestra, are based in Glasgow, they regularly come to Edinburgh to stage performances. The **Usher Hall** (ⓦ www.usherhall.co.uk) on Lothian Road is the main venue in the city for classical music, jazz and pop concerts, and is also responsible for the programme of events at the **Ross Open Air Theatre** (ⓣ (0131) 228 8616), which sits beneath the castle in Princes Street Gardens. But it is theatre that is the mainstay of Edinburgh's performing prowess.

The **Edinburgh Playhouse** (ⓐ 18–22 Greenside Place ⓣ (0131) 524 3333 ⓦ www.edinburghplayhouse.org.uk), the city's leading theatre, at the top of Leith Walk, is the main venue for touring high-glitz West End productions, predominantly musicals such as *Mamma Mia!* and *My Fair Lady*.

The modern **Festival Theatre** (ⓐ 13–29 Nicolson Street ⓣ (0131) 662 1112 ⓦ www.eft.co.uk) is a touch more conventionally cultural and presents a year-round programme of drama, opera and ballet, while dyed-in-the-wool luvvies will prefer the **King's Theatre**

Edinburgh Playhouse

in the city's West End district (2 Leven Street (0131) 529 6000 www.eft.co.uk), a smaller venue that stages touring repertory productions, including pantomime at Christmas. Edinburgh's own repertory theatre, the **Royal Lyceum Theatre** (30B Grindlay Street (0131) 248 4848 www.lyceum.org.uk), presents a variety of drama genres, with a strong emphasis on Scottish playwrights, while for cutting-edge work from home and abroad, the best place to go is the **Traverse Theatre** (10 Cambridge Street (0131) 228 1404 www.traverse.co.uk).

Most of Edinburgh's art galleries are in the New Town and Dean Village (see page 84) and present the finest collection of art in Scotland, ranging from traditional to modern conceptual genres. In addition to viewing art, there are many opportunities to buy, from the small and eclectic galleries in the Stockbridge area, to fine art galleries on Dundas Street in the New Town, to the annual

Edinburgh Art Fair that takes place each November at the Corn Exchange on Newmarket Road.

It could be said – in a positive sense – that much of Edinburgh itself is a museum, particularly the Old Town, where visitors live and breathe its history and which is now a World Heritage Site. The city's finest museum, truly world-class in terms of style, presentation and content, is the **National Museum of Scotland** (see page 75), which details the city's national heritage from prehistoric times to the present day. This is what a museum should be. But there are also more quirky attractions such as **The Real Mary King's Close** (see page 50) and **Gladstone's Land** (ⓐ 477B Lawnmarket, Royal Mile ⓣ (031) 226 5856), which explore how Edinburghers lived in tenement conditions for centuries, and offer the visitor more of a living history atmosphere. The castle (see page 64) has unique exhibitions, with the Scottish Crown Jewels as its highlight. Nature is the theme of two excellent 'museums': **Dynamic Earth** (see page 62) explores all manner of ever more relevant geological and ecological issues to do with the planet, while outside the city centre is the award-winning **Scottish Seabird Centre** (see page 125), which examines the area's natural avian world.

Three great Scottish writers – Robert Burns, Robert Louis Stevenson and Sir Walter Scott – are celebrated at the **Writers' Museum** (see page 75); indeed, Edinburgh is a hotbed of literary references, from Ian Rankin's Rebus stories, to Muriel Spark's Jean Brodie and the working-class Leith of Irvine Welsh's *Trainspotting*. There are many literary tours in the city taking visitors past places such as the site of the café where J K Rowling invented Harry Potter (now a Chinese restaurant) as well as pub crawls with literary associations (ⓦ www.edinburghliterarypubtour.co.uk).

Princes Street Gardens are a green escape right in the heart of the city

MAKING THE MOST OF
Edinburgh

Shopping

Edinburgh is something of a shopper's paradise, whether you're after designer names in fashion or textiles, one-off pieces from the many quirky boutiques, or simply classic Scottish souvenirs such as tartan, cashmere or whisky.

The Royal Mile (see page 71) is the place to head for if you're after traditional Scottish goods, although beware of the overly touristy shops, particularly those closest to the castle. Along this stretch of the Old Town you'll find innumerable shops selling all manner of tartan, luxurious cashmere sweaters and traditional edibles such as shortbread and fudge, in tartan-patterned tins. This is also a good place to find Celtic-styled jewellery and, for children, plastic swords and helmets as a nod to the country's warrior past.

Just off the Royal Mile is Cockburn Street, which is well known for its slightly alternative atmosphere, with second-hand clothes, books and record stores, as well as tattoo parlours and the like.

For upmarket designer names, you can't do better than St Andrew Square and Multrees Walk in the heart of the New Town, where you'll find the luxury of Harvey Nichols (see page 93) and an elegant pedestrianised street. Just along from here is George Street, where slightly cheaper but equally stylish names can be found. One-off stylish boutiques are a speciality of the lovely Thistle Street, also in the New Town. The classic Edinburgh department store is Jenners (see page 93), which has a slightly old-fashioned feel to it but is still the shop of choice for most well-to-do Edinburgh ladies.

Princes Street is the most famous shopping street in Edinburgh, but without just cause in terms of retail value. It's little more than a mile-long cluster of everyday high-street stores. Come for the

A traditional Edinburgh shopfront

LOCAL CRAFTS

Within Edinburgh itself, the Tartan Weaving Mill (see page 51) and the Scotch Whisky Experience (see page 51) are the best places to go for a weave or a dram.

Outside Edinburgh are two further craft centres well worth a visit. The **Glenkinchie Distillery** (ⓐ Pencaitland, Tranent ⓣ (01875) 342 004 ⓦ www.discovering-distilleries.com/glenkinchie), 24 km (15 miles) from the city, also offers the opportunity to learn about the distillation of malt whiskies and buy samples to take home. An hour from Edinburgh, in the heart of the Borders, is **Hawick Knitwear** (ⓐ Liddesdale Road, Hawick ⓣ (01450) 363 100), where the factory shop sells the traditional woollen designs for which Scotland is famed.

view, but in terms of shopping you won't find anything here that you couldn't find at home.

The antiques areas of the city are Grassmarket and West Bow in the Old Town and Dundas Street in the New Town, as well as along Causewayside in southern Edinburgh. If you're looking for a piece of art to take home, Stockbridge is the area with the most attractive small galleries.

The main market in Edinburgh is the farmers' market (see page 76), held each Saturday near the castle.

Given Edinburgh's unreliable weather, the city does have its fair share of covered shopping centres, although few offer anything exclusive. The most central of these is the **Princes Street Mall** (ⓐ Princes Street ⓣ (0131) 557 3759 ⓦ www.princesmall-edinburgh.co.uk), which is rather dull in nature but does at least have all the standard

British high-street shops. In Leith the **Ocean Terminal** (see page 106) is attempting to follow the lead of the area's successful regeneration. Although very smart, it is, however, a little soulless and not worth the trip to this area of town simply for shopping purposes.

The largest shopping centre is on the outskirts of the city. **Fort Kinnaird Shopping Complex** (ⓐ Newcraighall Road ⓣ (0131) 669 9090) covers 54,000 sq m (581,000 sq ft) and includes all the major names as well as numerous cafés and fast-food outlets.

Tartan cloth on sale in Edinburgh

Eating & drinking

Edinburgh has a range of top-class restaurants, fashionable cafés and bars, as well as a wide selection of budget options. Pub culture is alive and well, and the advantage here is that traditional has not often given way to soulless modern design. Many of the pubs remain as they have been for the past 100 years. For those who prefer a more funky feel, however, there are glitzy bars here too, particularly in areas such as George Street in the New Town.

The opening hours of Edinburgh's pubs, bars and clubs can be a vexed and shifting question. By law, venues with a licence to sell alcohol may do so to anyone aged 18 or over, 24 hours a day. Few of them actually open 24/7, but do bear in mind that opening hours can fluctuate widely, and deviate from stated times, not least during the period of The Festival and Fringe (see page 14), when it's not unusual for bars and pubs to stay open until five in the morning (and open again at six). The opening hours in this guide are the official hours provided by the venues themselves, but be prepared for them to change without warning.

As would be expected, many of the restaurants and cafés in the Old Town, particularly along the Royal Mile, are either tourist traps

PRICE CATEGORIES

The following price guide used throughout the book indicates the average price per head for a two- to three-course à la carte dinner, excluding drinks. Lunch will usually be a little cheaper and many restaurants also offer fixed-price menus.

£ up to £20 **££** £20–30 **£££** over £30

or uninteresting chains, but a few gems can be found away from the main streets. The New Town, however, is the heart of fine dining in the city, while Leith, unsurprisingly, has a string of highly lauded fish and seafood restaurants with the added advantage of sea views.

Stop for a break in an old café with a view of the castle

Scottish restaurants focus heavily on meat and fish, although vegetarians should always be able to find a suitable option. In addition there are plenty of ethnic restaurants around the city, including Chinese and Indian, which always offer plenty of vegetarian choices.

There's no hard and fast rule as to whether restaurants include service charges on their bill or not – some do and some don't – so check your bill when paying. If service is not included, it's customary to leave a tip of 10–15 per cent of the cost of the meal. Tips aren't required in pubs if you're only drinking.

All public places, including restaurants, pubs and bars, are strictly non-smoking.

The Saturday farmers' market by the castle (see page 76) is a great place to pick up Scottish specialities, and if you're lucky enough to have a sunny day, it's ideal for picnic foods. The food hall of Harvey Nichols (see page 93) is a more luxurious option, while the city is scattered

A traditional Scottish pub in Leith

with delis and speciality shops where you can pick up a selection of tasty Scottish cheeses.

In terms of specialities, haggis is probably the most famous Scottish dish. Similar to a ball-shaped sausage, it consists of sheep's intestines, heart and liver, minced with onion, oatmeal and various spices, contained within the animal's stomach lining, then boiled and traditionally served with 'neeps and tatties' (mashed swede and potato). If the real thing doesn't appeal, vegetarian haggis made with pulses, vegetables and nuts is increasingly available, although most Scots find the notion an aberration.

Meat plays an important part in Scottish cuisine and you'll see plenty of Aberdeen Angus beef, venison and lamb on restaurant menus, and game such as pheasant and partridge in season. Given the city's coastal location, fish and seafood are also abundant, and oyster lovers will never go wanting. Cullen Skink is a delicious haddock and potato soup that is very heartening on a cold winter's day, while Arbroath Smokies are smoked haddock that originate from the coastal town about 160 km (100 miles) north of the capital. And, of course, fish and chips of high quality are available all over the city.

For a savoury snack many bakers sell bridies, which are a take on the Cornish pasty but made with plain instead of puff pastry, and filled with minced beef and onions. Another savoury snack is oatcakes, delicious when served with Scottish cheeses. For a sweet tea-time snack you can't go wrong with traditional Scottish shortbread.

Whisky is the most famous Scottish drink, both malt and blended, made in distilleries around the country. Edinburgh also has its own brewery, the Caledonian, which produces popular ales such as 80 Shilling, named after the original cost of the barrel. Scotland's home-produced soft drink is Irn Bru (pronounced 'Iron Brew'), a bright orange fizzy concoction that people either love or hate.

Entertainment & nightlife

Edinburgh takes entertainment and nightlife very seriously indeed, although the emphasis tends towards cultural good times rather than bare-faced hedonism. Jazz clubs thrive here and nightclubs have a sophisticated edge to them, although anyone looking for a more grungy atmosphere will find plenty of options in the Old Town and West End areas. Tickets for most venues are available at the door.

As the location for many top-rated films, such as *The Prime of Miss Jean Brodie* and *Trainspotting*, as well as being the birthplace of Hollywood legend Sean Connery, it's not surprising that Edinburgh is a film-loving city. It has its fair share of cinema chains and a handful of specialist film venues.

The Cameo (ⓐ 38 Home Street ⓣ (0871) 902 5723), Edinburgh's art-house film venue, is in a historic building that dates from 1914. There's also a bar, and drinks can be taken into the screening area. **The Filmhouse** (ⓐ 88 Lothian Road ⓣ (0131) 228 2688 ⓦ www.filmhousecinema.com) is a regional cinema that's home to the annual Edinburgh International Film Festival (see page 13) and also screens popular general releases (but not blockbusters), as well as art-house films and documentaries. In the **Omni Centre**, at the top of Leith Walk (ⓐ Omni Centre, Greenside Place ⓣ (08712) 240 240), there is a 12-screen cinema complex showing all the latest releases, while the Ocean Terminal complex in Leith (see page 106) is another multiplex offering.

Edinburgh has a strong tradition of stand-up comedy. The Festival's if.comedy Award (formerly the Perrier Award, see page 14) put it firmly on the British map. **Highlight** (ⓐ 28 Greenside Row ⓣ (0844) 844 0044 ⓦ www.thehighlight.co.uk), part of a chain of comedy clubs, presents comedians every Friday and Saturday night, while

Traditional highland dancers are always present at Scottish festivals

WHAT'S ON

Edinburgh's main listings magazine (which also covers Glasgow) is the weekly *The List*, available from the tourist office and most newsagents. As well as articles about events relevant to both cities, it gives full listings of club nights, cinemas, theatre, gay events and comedy. It also has an online source, ⓦ www.list.co.uk

The Stand Comedy Club (ⓐ 5 York Place ⓣ (0131) 558 7272 ⓦ www.thestand.co.uk), one of the best-known comedy clubs in Britain, has high-quality performances seven nights a week.

The city has a very healthy live music scene. The annual Jazz and Blues Festival (see page 9) draws big names from around the world, but many jazz clubs around the city are full to the rafters with cool cats listening to dulcet tones throughout the year. Jools Holland has had a great success with his Jam House (see page 97) in the New Town, and the Scottish National Jazz Orchestra is also based here. For a purely Scottish feel, however, don't miss the many folk-music events, a great deal of which are impromptu musical get-togethers in bars. Local well-known bands such as The Proclaimers regularly play in Edinburgh and shouldn't be missed if one of their gigs coincides with your visit. If you want to dance as well as listen, the **Assembly Rooms** (ⓐ 54 George Street ⓣ (0131) 220 4348 ⓦ www.assemblyroomsedinburgh.co.uk) hold regular ceilidhs, the traditional Scottish folk-dancing evenings.

While not so much of a clubbing city as its western neighbour Glasgow, Edinburgh nevertheless has a thriving scene, both straight and gay, and attracts many big-name DJs from the rest of the country.

One of the main clubbing areas is Cowgate, which can become rowdy and unpleasant in the early hours of Saturday and Sunday. Traditionally Rose Street has been the main pub-crawling area of the city, although George Street, running parallel behind it, has smarter options. The main gay area is at the top of Leith Walk.

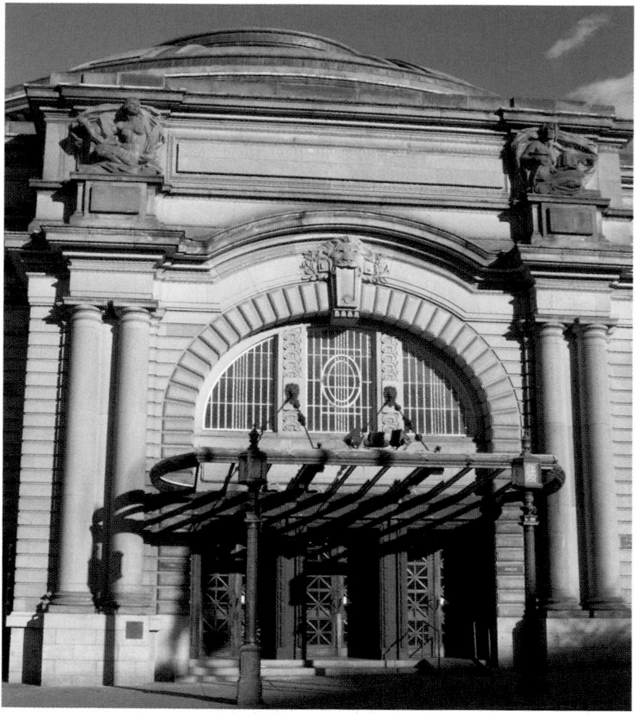

The Usher Hall is a popular live-music venue

Sport & relaxation

SPECTATOR SPORTS

Football Football is the main spectator sport in Edinburgh, with strong competition between Edinburgh's two major clubs, Hearts (Heart of Midlothian, ⓦ www.heartsfc.co.uk) and Hibs (Hibernian, ⓦ www.hibernianfc.co.uk). Hearts' home ground is Tynecastle on Gorgie Road, and match tickets can be obtained from their website, while Hibernian play at the Easter Road Stadium, with tickets available by telephoning ⓣ (0131) 661 1875. There's a long-standing rivalry between the two clubs, much of it historical and sectarian, with Hearts traditionally Protestant and Hibs Catholic, but it's largely harmless.

Easter Road Stadium ⓐ 12 Albion Place ⓣ (0131) 661 2159
Tynecastle Stadium ⓐ Gorgie Road ⓣ (0131) 200 7200

Horse racing Horse racing is popular here, and there are 26 race meetings, both flat racing and jump racing, as well as speciality events such as Mardi Gras, at the Musselburgh Racecourse along the coast from the city centre. Tickets can be booked on the course's website.

Musselburgh Racecourse ⓐ Linkfield Road, Musselburgh ⓣ (0131) 665 2859 ⓦ www.musselburgh-racecourse.co.uk

Rugby Edinburgh has several rugby teams, including the professional Edinburgh Gunners (ⓦ www.edinburghgunners.org.uk). Rugby Union games are played at weekends at the historic Murrayfield Stadium to the west of the city, off Roseburn Street. Tickets are elusive, but telephone ⓣ (0131) 346 5250 for more information.

Murrayfield Stadium ⓦ www.murrayfieldexperience.com

PARTICIPATION SPORTS

Golf Of the six courses near the game's home town, the most central is the nine-holer at Portobello; the most challenging is the par 71 at Braid Hills.

Braid Hills 91 Liberton Drive (0131) 658 1111

Portobello Golf Course Stanley Street (0131) 669 4361

Sailing There are plenty of opportunities for messing about on the water in and around Edinburgh, including kayaking, dinghy sailing and powerboating. The company **Edinburgh Leisure** (Vantage Point, 3 Cultins Road (0131) 458 2100 www.edinburghleisure.co.uk) organises a variety of trips and courses.

Skiing Midlothian Snowsports Centre at Hill End is the nearest skiing opportunity to the city, only 4 km (2½ miles) away, and the slope can be seen from various parts of Edinburgh. But it's only dry skiing, even if it is the longest dry slope in Britain. For the nearest snow skiing head for Glenshee Ski Centre, about 100 km (62 miles) north of Edinburgh near Braemar.

Glenshee Ski Centre Cairnwell, Braemar (013397) 41320 www.ski-glenshee.co.uk

Midlothian Snowsports Centre Biggar Road (0131) 445 4433

RELAXATION

Walking & hiking For a gentle hill walk within the city itself, explore the mound of Arthur's Seat (see page 70), with its well-maintained footpaths. Further afield, **Walk Scotland** (www.walkscotland.com) organises a 19-km (12-mile) hike in the Pentland Hills (see page 125), one of Scotland's regional parks, with great opportunities for birdwatching and wonderful views.

Accommodation

Like most British cities, Edinburgh has accommodation to suit all budgets, from the ultra-luxurious to basic lodgings and motels, to quaint B&Bs both in and outside the city. Some hotels include breakfast in the room rate and some don't, so check before you book. In the larger hotels breakfast is likely to be a full Scottish breakfast, including black pudding and haggis.

HOTELS

Davenport House Hotel £ A traditionally decorated guesthouse in a converted Georgian building, offering a far more luxurious feel than the price tag would suggest. ⓐ 58 Great King Street ⓣ (0131) 558 8495 ⓦ http://davenport-house.com

Elder York Guest House £ Centrally situated on the eastern edge of the New Town with friendly and helpful staff, comfortable rooms and an excellent Scottish breakfast. ⓐ 38 Elder Street ⓣ (0131) 556 1926 ⓦ www.elderyork.co.uk

Ibis Edinburgh Centre £ Another great location for a great price, just off the Royal Mile and with parking. ⓐ 6 Hunter Square ⓣ (0870) 765 5094 ⓦ www.ibishotel.com

PRICE CATEGORIES

The following ratings indicate the average price per double room per night – some rooms may be more or less expensive than the rating suggests, depending on high or low season.

£ up to £90 **££** £90–150 **£££** over £150

Travelodge Edinburgh Central £ Don't expect any frills here, but for its location in the heart of the Old Town, and price, it can't be beaten. ⓐ 12 St Mary's Street ⓣ (0871) 984 6137 ⓦ www.travelodge.co.uk

The Bonham ££ Affordable luxury in the West End at one of Edinburgh's most popular hotels. All rooms are individually decorated in contemporary style. The restaurant serves French cuisine. ⓐ 35 Drumsheugh Gardens ⓣ (0131) 226 6050 ⓦ www.townhousecompany.com

Malmaison ££ The landmark Leith hotel overlooking the waterfront and set in a former Victorian seamen's mission. Inside, everything is minimally designed, with bold shapes in muted tones. ⓐ 1 Tower Place ⓣ (0845) 45 66 399 ⓦ www.malmaison-edinburgh.com

Mount Royal Ramada Jarvis ££ A good mid-range option for its central location with a wonderful view of the castle, although its chain-hotel atmosphere is a little bland. ⓐ 53 Princes Street ⓣ (0844) 815 9017 ⓦ www.ramadajarvis.co.uk

The Point Hotel ££ One of the finest design hotels in the world – or so its promotion claims. A feel of Manhattan about it, with fluorescent-coloured lighting, black-and-white rooms and wonderful castle views. ⓐ 34 Bread Street ⓣ (0131) 221 5555 ⓦ www.mercure.com

Rick's ££ A lovely boutique hotel with only ten en-suite rooms. The minimalist rooms include angora blankets, soft towelling robes and DVD players. The restaurant has a terrace outside and is open from 07.30 until late. ⓐ 55A Frederick Street ⓣ (0131) 622 7800 ⓦ www.ricksedinburgh.co.uk

Six Mary's Place ££ In the arty atmosphere of Stockbridge, this is a lovely converted house decorated in muted pastel shades while retaining original Georgian details. Great value. ⓐ Raeburn Place ⓣ (0131) 332 8965 ⓦ www.sixmarysplace.co.uk

The Balmoral £££ Part of the Rocco Forte chain, this is the place to stay if money is no object. All the en-suite rooms are styled to perfection while the restaurant has earnt itself a Michelin star. There's also a pool and health club. ⓐ 1 Princes Street ⓣ (0131) 556 2414 ⓦ www.thebalmoralhotel.com

The Caledonian Hilton £££ An Edinburgh institution with 250 rooms, many with castle views, a health club and central location on the corner of Princes Street. ⓐ Princes Street ⓣ (0131) 222 8888 ⓦ www.hilton.co.uk/caledonian

The Carlton £££ Convenient for the Royal Mile and the castle, The Carlton is a famous Edinburgh institution, although it is slightly lacking in the personal touch. ⓐ North Bridge ⓣ (0131) 472 3000 ⓦ www.barcelo-hotels.co.uk

Dalhousie Castle £££ About half an hour's drive from the city centre, staying in this converted 13th-century castle is worth it for a special occasion. The cellar restaurant is superb, serving the finest Scottish food. ⓐ Bonnyrigg ⓣ (01875) 820 153 ⓦ www.dalhousiecastle.co.uk

The George £££ Set in a listed building and ornately decorated with chandeliers, velvet curtains and original tiles, many of the rooms here have views of the castle. This is possibly the finest

The Michelin-starred Balmoral

hotel in town. ⓐ 19–21 George Street ⓣ (0131) 225 1251 ⓦ www.edinburghgeorgehotel.co.uk

Hotel Missoni £££ The famous Italian fashion house has chosen Edinburgh as the location for its first UK hotel and, as you'd expect, its décor is all high-end design contrasting black and white with the company's well-known colourful stripes. Definitely the hippest place to stay in the heart of the city. ⓐ 1 George IV Bridge ⓣ (0131) 220 6666 ⓦ www.hotelmissoni.com

Number Ten Hotel £££ In a beautiful Georgian building in the New Town, the Number Ten combines classic charm with modern style. ⓐ 10 Gloucester Place ⓣ (0131) 225 2720 ⓦ www.numbertenhotel.com

Radisson Blu Hotel Edinburgh £££ An excellent location on the Royal Mile and also benefiting from a car park (for a small fee). The health spa, including pool and sauna, is ideal for soothing cobble-tired feet. ⓐ 80 High Street, Royal Mile ⓣ (0131) 473 6590 ⓦ www.radissonblu.co.uk

The Scotsman £££ Housed in the impressive former *Scotsman* newspaper building, this is an elegant option that also benefits from its own high-tech spa and excellent restaurant. ⓐ 20 North Bridge ⓣ (0131) 556 5565 ⓦ www.theetoncollection.co.uk

CAMPING

Edinburgh Caravan Club Site £ To the north of the city on the Firth of Forth, caravans and tents are both accepted in what is the most convenient area for the city centre. ⓐ Marine Drive ⓣ (0131) 312 6874

Mortonhall Caravan & Camping Park £ This country estate has caravans to let and pitches for tents, as well as communal bathing facilities, a laundry and a games room. ⓐ 38 Mortonhall Gate, Frogston Road East ⓣ (0131) 664 1533 ⓦ www.meadowhead.co.uk

Tantallon Caravan Park ££ Outside the city at North Berwick is this lovely park with sea views and a golf course. Both tent camping and caravanning are available. ⓐ Dunbar Road, North Berwick ⓣ (01620) 893 348 ⓦ www.meadowhead.co.uk

SELF-CATERING

Edinburgh Self-Catering ££–£££ This company provides various apartments in the city centre, mostly in the Old Town. ⓐ 3 The Cross, Pencaitland ⓣ (01875) 341 490 ⓦ www.edinburgh-selfcatering.co.uk

The Chester Residence £££ If you want 5-star luxury without the hotel feel, these five apartments are the choice for you. Beautifully decorated with full attention to detail, you can cater for yourself but won't have to worry about clearing up as the apartments are serviced daily. ⓐ 9 Chester Street ⓣ (0131) 226 2075 ⓦ www.chester-residence.com

YOUTH HOSTELS

The most central hostel in Edinburgh, as its name suggests, is **Edinburgh Central** (ⓐ 9 Haddington Place ⓣ (0131) 524 2090) at the top of Leith Walk. **Budget Backpackers** (ⓣ (0131) 226 6351 ⓦ www.budgetbackpackers.co.uk) has up-to-the-second information on hostel room availability in the city.

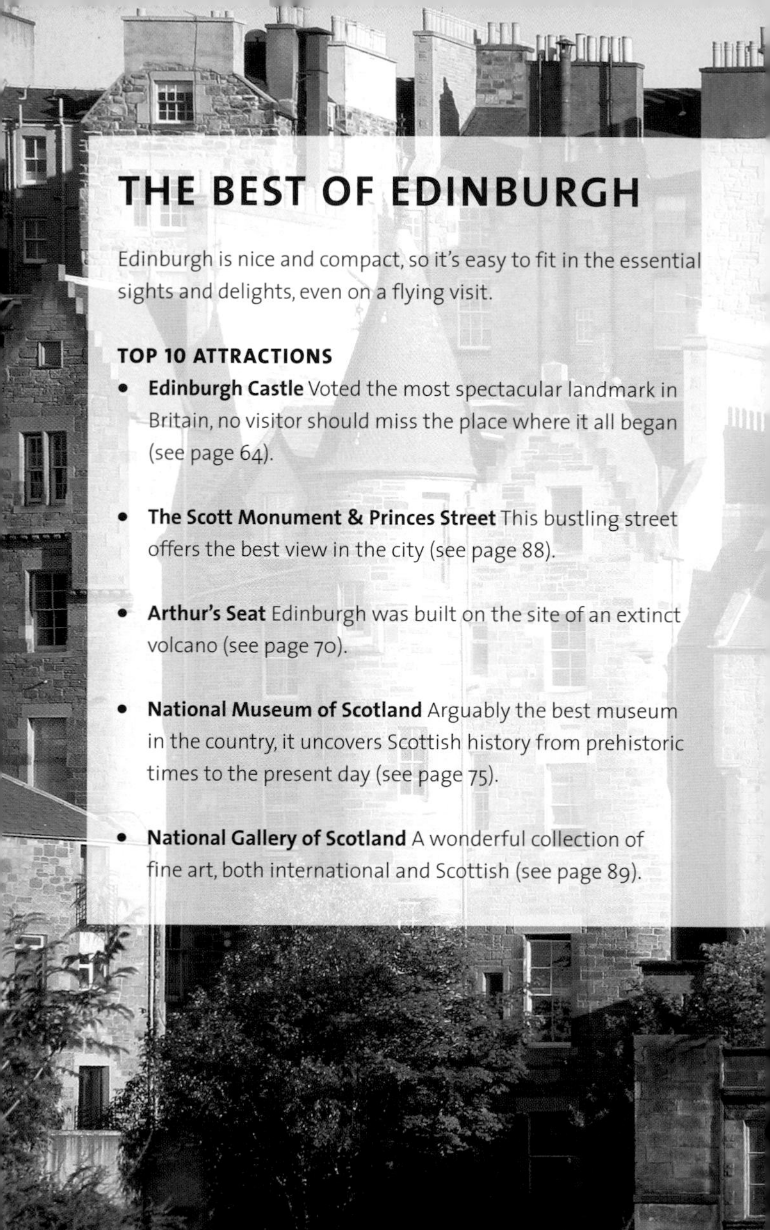

THE BEST OF EDINBURGH

Edinburgh is nice and compact, so it's easy to fit in the essential sights and delights, even on a flying visit.

TOP 10 ATTRACTIONS

- **Edinburgh Castle** Voted the most spectacular landmark in Britain, no visitor should miss the place where it all began (see page 64).
- **The Scott Monument & Princes Street** This bustling street offers the best view in the city (see page 88).
- **Arthur's Seat** Edinburgh was built on the site of an extinct volcano (see page 70).
- **National Museum of Scotland** Arguably the best museum in the country, it uncovers Scottish history from prehistoric times to the present day (see page 75).
- **National Gallery of Scotland** A wonderful collection of fine art, both international and Scottish (see page 89).

- **The Palace of Holyroodhouse** Still the official royal residence in Scotland, the highlight here is the apartments of Mary, Queen of Scots (see page 69).

- **Edinburgh International & Fringe Festival** The largest arts festival in the world takes over the city every August (see page 14).

- **Edinburgh Military Tattoo** A spectacular performance by the Scottish regiments and international regimental guests in front of the castle every August (see page 10).

- **The Royal Mile** Leading from the castle to the palace, this cobbled street is the hub of the Old Town with innumerable sights along its route (see page 71).

- **Calton Hill** This replica of the Greek Parthenon, high on a hill overlooking the New Town, confirmed Edinburgh's nickname 'Athens of the North' (see page 82).

The historic stone buildings of Edinburgh

Suggested itineraries

HALF-DAY: EDINBURGH IN A HURRY

If you're pressed for time but want a little exploration, head straight for the Royal Mile (see page 71), taking in the atmosphere of this medieval cobbled street, and walk up to the castle. Admire the views from the ramparts, marvel at its precarious cliff-top position, and go inside to uncover the history of the Scottish monarchy and the city.

1 DAY: TIME TO SEE A LITTLE MORE

If you have more time, you can appreciate the two contrasting aspects of the city: the medieval and the Georgian. From the Royal Mile walk over North Bridge into Princes Street to admire the views and visit the National Gallery of Scotland (see page 89). Then walk around the streets behind it, such as George, Queen, Dublin and Dundas Streets, to admire the Georgian architecture for which the city is so renowned.

2–3 DAYS: TIME TO SEE MUCH MORE

Explore almost all aspects of this wonderful city. Enjoy a waterside drink in Leith and witness the successful regeneration of the once-rundown docklands area. Take in the arty atmosphere of Stockbridge, then stroll along the Water of Leith to Dean Village to visit the Dean Gallery (see page 89) and the wonderful work of the Scottish sculptor Eduardo Paolozzi. Weather permitting, walk up to the peak of Arthur's Seat (see page 70) to experience a taste of the wilderness right in the heart of the capital.

LONGER: ENJOYING EDINBURGH TO THE FULL

With added time you can revisit some of the areas to take in more sights, such as the Scottish National Portrait Gallery (see page 90)

and the Royal Botanic Gardens in the New Town (see page 87) or the National Museum of Scotland in the Old Town (see page 75). You could also take a journey out to the Borders and Firth of Forth region, enjoying the wildness of Gullane beach or exploring the mysterious Rosslyn Chapel (see page 138), 9 km (5½ miles) south of the city.

Views of the Forth from Arthur's Seat

Something for nothing

Edinburgh is not a particularly expensive city and entrance to all its museums is free, except for special exhibitions. However, there are plenty of other ways to take in the city without having to thrust your hand into your sporran-style purse.

The **National Library of Scotland** (ⓐ 57 George IV Bridge ⓣ (0131) 623 3700 ⓦ www.nls.uk) is the largest library in the country

Arthur's Seat

THE EDINBURGH PASS

If you're in the city for only a short time and want to cram in every sightseeing possibility, it is worth buying the Edinburgh Pass, available for one-, two- or three-day periods. Although it's an initial cost, it does then gain you free bus travel and free entrance into more than 25 attractions, including Dynamic Earth (see page 62), themed tours and any special exhibitions going on in the galleries or museums, as well as discounts in many shops and restaurants. For details, see Ⓦ www.edinburgh.org/pass

and has a fantastic collection of rare books, manuscripts, maps and other items relating to Scottish history and culture. Of particular interest is the collection of traditional Scottish music.

For those who like to walk, through either urban or natural landscapes, few cities offer so many opportunities. Within the city the Water of Leith (see page 87) is a lovely stroll along the riverbank where various waterbirds can be spotted. The Royal Botanic Gardens (see page 87) are a draw for budding horticulturalists, particularly in spring when the daffodils and many other plants come into bloom. For those with a head for heights, climb to the top of Calton Hill (see page 82) to see the Parthenon and the Nelson Monument as well as great views of the New Town, or for a more wild experience ascend Arthur's Seat (see page 70) and the Salisbury Crags, where, on a clear day, you'll have an enviable view across the Forth to Fife. Take advantage of Edinburgh's coastal location by either exploring the urban style of The Shore in Leith or head out to Portobello for a walk along the sandy beach, a favourite with the city's dog owners.

When it rains

Sad to say, it's likely that most visitors will experience a spot of rain during a trip to Edinburgh, particularly in autumn and winter, but there are numerous attractions that are fascinating in their own right and that will protect you from outside downpours, aside from the various museums and galleries.

Those with an artistic leaning can escape the weather by visiting **Trinity Apse** (ⓐ Chalmers Close, High Street, Royal Mile ⓣ (0131) 556 4364) on the Royal Mile and viewing those who perform brass rubbing on the church's medieval brasses. Staff are *in situ* to show you what to do, and if the bug bites, there are also kits on sale. Do note, though, that there is a small charge for those who want to have a go at rubbing. You might not have considered the **Camera Obscura** (ⓐ Castlehill, Royal Mile ⓣ (0131) 226 3709 ⓦ www.camera-obscura.co.uk) as a rainy-day option; the rooftop terrace may be outside, but inside are plenty of attractions displaying optical illusions and tricks, including holograms, 3-D images of Edinburgh, as well as the camera itself, where you can 'spy' on the city in secret.

A little social history is always good for the soul, so why not take the opportunity to have a poke around **The Real Mary King's Close** (ⓐ 2 Warriston's Close, High Street, Royal Mile ⓣ (0845) 070 6244 ⓦ www.realmarykingsclose.com). Edinburgh's closes were high-rise tenements with dire living conditions. For centuries the former homes lay hidden beneath the city but they have been opened as a tourist attraction. Guides in costumes and character take visitors through a series of dark, dusty chambers to reveal just how squalid life here could be, as well as narrating the story of some of the inhabitants.

A nice length of fabric does much to lift drab-weather blues, and as you'll see tartan adorning everything from teddy bears to slippers along the Royal Mile, step out of the rain and into the **Tartan Weaving Mill** (ⓐ 555 Castlehill, Royal Mile ⓣ (0131) 226 1555) to see how it's made. Watch the weavers at work at their power looms, learn about clan tartans and dress up in Highland costume, before deciding whether you want to buy some tartan to take home with you.

Very close to the Tartan Weaving Mill, the **Scotch Whisky Experience** (ⓐ 354 Castlehill, Royal Mile ⓣ (0131) 220 0441 ⓦ www.whisky-heritage.co.uk) uncovers the history of another great Scottish tradition. There's a model distillery, a journey back in time via dioramas riding on a whisky 'barrel' on tracks, and an explanation of the different malt whiskies and where they are made. Perhaps most importantly, there's a well-stocked shop where you can pick up a bottle or two to take home.

The Scotch Whisky Experience on the Royal Mile

On arrival

TIME DIFFERENCE

Edinburgh's clocks follow Greenwich Mean Time (GMT). During Daylight Saving Time (end Mar–end Oct) the clocks are put forward one hour.

ARRIVING

By air

Edinburgh International Airport (t (0844) 481 8989 w www.edinburghairport.com) is 8 km (5 miles) from the city centre and an efficient Air Link coach connects the two for the 20-minute journey. There are also plenty of taxis for a higher cost. There are flights between Edinburgh and London and many other British cities every day, as well as flights to many European cities. There is also a daily flight between Edinburgh and New York, but for more international flights **Glasgow Airport** (t (0844) 481 5555 w www.glasgowairport.com), an hour away from Edinburgh, is a better option.

By rail

Train services into **Edinburgh Waverley Station** (t (0131) 550 2031) are handled by **East Coast** (w www.eastcoast.co.uk), **Virgin** (w www.virgintrains.co.uk) and **ScotRail** (w www.scotrail.co.uk). There are daily services between London and Edinburgh making the journey in around four and a half hours, as well as direct links to York, Lancaster and Newcastle in England, and Aberdeen, Glasgow and Inverness in Scotland. To find out about timetables and fares contact **National Rail Enquiries** (t (08457) 48 49 50 w www.nationalrail.co.uk).

By road

Coaches run by **National Express** (t (08717) 81 81 78 w www.nationalexpress.com) link Edinburgh with various UK and Scottish cities and are a great budget option for getting to the city.

Edinburgh is at the centre of a spider's web of motorways and A roads, including the M1/A1 coastal route from London. Coming from the west of England the M6/M74 is the best route to both Edinburgh and Glasgow. The city is directly linked to Glasgow via the M8. The journey time by road between London and Edinburgh is about eight hours.

By water

An overnight **Norfolkline** ferry (t (0871) 230 0330 w www.norfolkline.com) operates between Zeebrugge in Belgium and Rosyth, just north of the city centre, with a crossing time of 17 hours.

FINDING YOUR FEET

Edinburgh has been voted one of the safest cities in Europe, so no visitor should feel any sense of threat, although like everywhere, in crowded tourist spots pickpockets may be in operation so keep an eye on your belongings at all times. Traffic can be a problem in the centre so use the pedestrian crossings, wait for the green man to light up, and remember that traffic will be coming from the right not the left. Police officers, taxi drivers and locals, who are invariably friendly, will all help if you need to ask for directions.

ORIENTATION

The city centre is divided between two areas, the Old Town and the New Town, separated by the North and Waverley railway bridges. The main thoroughfare of the Old Town is the Royal Mile (High Street),

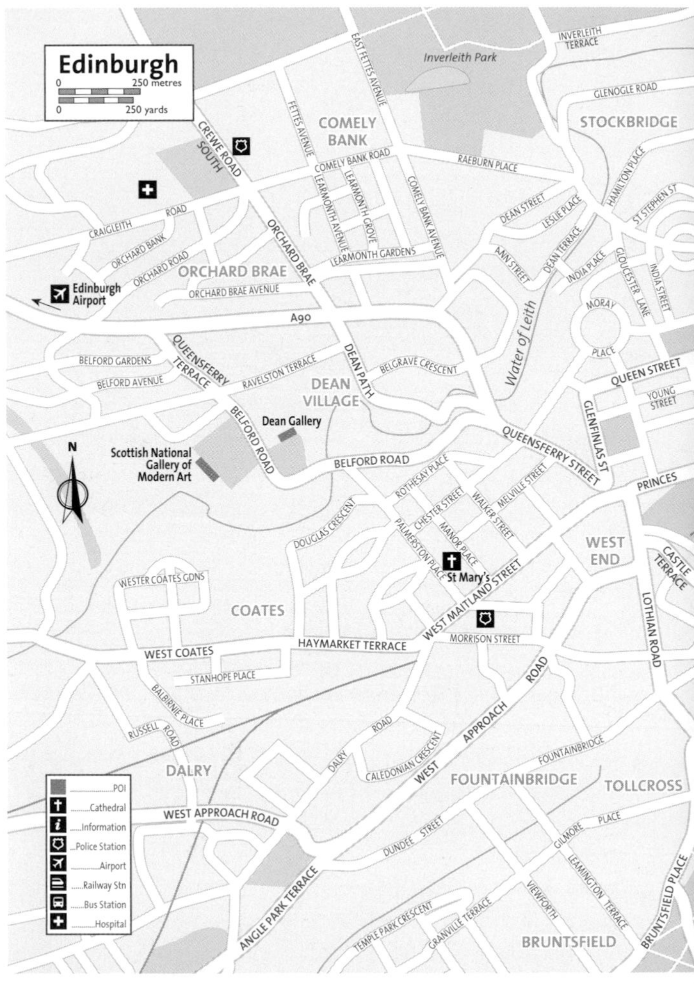
Edinburgh
0 250 metres
0 250 yards
Inverleith Park
INVERLEITH TERRACE
GLENOGLE ROAD
STOCKBRIDGE
COMELY BANK
EAST FETTES AVENUE
FETTES AVENUE
CREWE ROAD SOUTH
COMELY BANK ROAD
RAEBURN PLACE
LEARMONTH AVENUE
LEARMONTH GROVE
COMELY BANK AVENUE
LEARMONTH GARDENS
HAMILTON PLACE
ST STEPHEN ST
DEAN STREET
LESLIE PLACE
ANN STREET
DEAN TERRACE
INDIA PLACE
GLOUCESTER LANE
INDIA STREET
CRAIGLEITH ROAD
ORCHARD BANK
ORCHARD ROAD
ORCHARD BRAE
ORCHARD BRAE AVENUE
Edinburgh Airport
A90
MORAY PLACE
Water of Leith
QUEEN STREET
YOUNG STREET
BELFORD GARDENS
BELFORD AVENUE
QUEENSFERRY TERRACE
RAVELSTON TERRACE
DEAN PATH
BELGRAVE CRESCENT
DEAN VILLAGE
GLENFINLAS ST
Dean Gallery
BELFORD ROAD
N
Scottish National Gallery of Modern Art
QUEENSFERRY STREET
PRINCES
ROTHESAY PLACE
MELVILLE STREET
CHESTER STREET
WALKER STREET
DOUGLAS CRESCENT
PALMERSTON PLACE
MANOR PLACE
WEST END
CASTLE TERRACE
St Mary's
WESTER COATES GDNS
COATES
WEST MAITLAND STREET
LOTHIAN ROAD
MORRISON STREET
HAYMARKET TERRACE
WEST COATES
STANHOPE PLACE
BALBIRNIE PLACE
RUSSELL ROAD
DALRY ROAD
CALEDONIAN CRESCENT
WEST APPROACH ROAD
FOUNTAINBRIDGE
TOLLCROSS
DALRY
POI
Cathedral
Information
Police Station
Airport
Railway Stn
Bus Station
Hospital
DUNDEE STREET
GILMORE PLACE
LEAMINGTON TERRACE
VIEWFORTH
ANGLE PARK TERRACE
TEMPLE PARK CRESCENT
GRANVILLE TERRACE
BRUNTSFIELD
BRUNTSFIELD PLACE

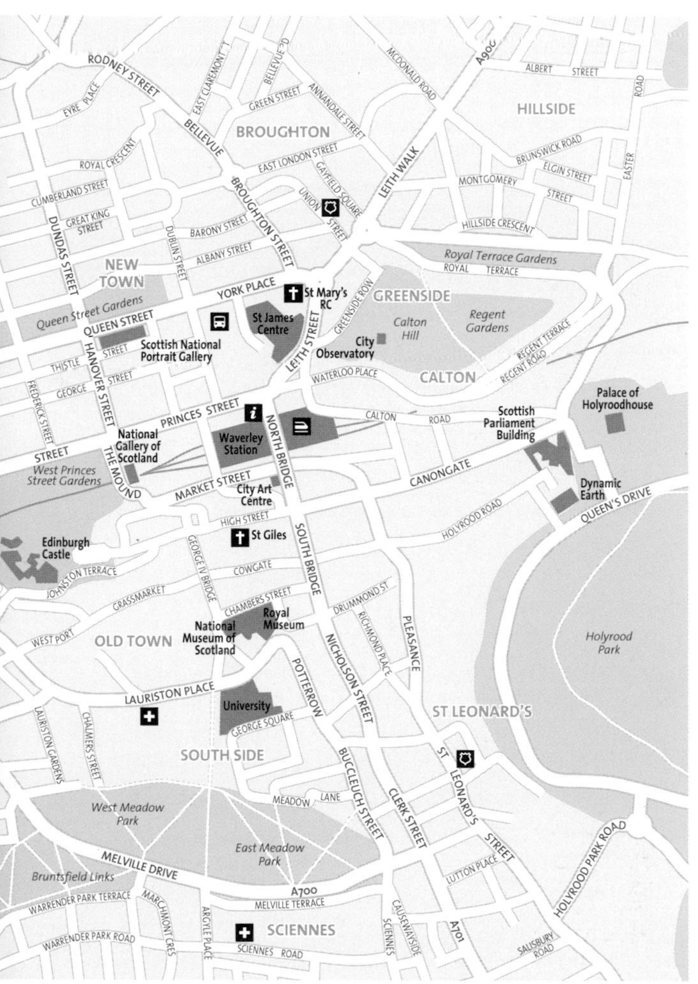
RODNEY STREET
EYRE PLACE
EAST CLAREMONT ST
BELLEVUE RD
GREEN STREET
ANNANDALE STREET
MCDONALD ROAD
A900
ALBERT STREET
ROAD
HILLSIDE
BROUGHTON
BELLEVUE
ROYAL CRESCENT
EAST LONDON STREET
GAYFIELD SQUARE
LEITH WALK
BRUNSWICK ROAD
ELGIN STREET
EASTER
CUMBERLAND STREET
GREAT KING STREET
BROUGHTON STREET
UNION STREET
MONTGOMERY STREET
HILLSIDE CRESCENT
DUNDAS STREET
DUBLIN STREET
BARONY STREET
ALBANY STREET
Royal Terrace Gardens
ROYAL TERRACE
NEW TOWN
YORK PLACE
St Mary's RC
GREENSIDE ROW
GREENSIDE
Queen Street Gardens
QUEEN STREET
St James Centre
LEITH STREET
Calton Hill
Regent Gardens
Scottish National Portrait Gallery
City Observatory
REGENT TERRACE
REGENT ROAD
THISTLE STREET
HANOVER STREET
FREDERICK STREET
GEORGE STREET
WATERLOO PLACE
CALTON
Palace of Holyroodhouse
PRINCES STREET
CALTON ROAD
Scottish Parliament Building
National Gallery of Scotland
Waverley Station
NORTH BRIDGE
STREET
West Princes Street Gardens
THE MOUND
MARKET STREET
City Art Centre
CANONGATE
Dynamic Earth
QUEEN'S DRIVE
HIGH STREET
HOLYROOD ROAD
St Giles
Edinburgh Castle
GEORGE IV BRIDGE
SOUTH BRIDGE
JOHNSTON TERRACE
COWGATE
GRASSMARKET
CHAMBERS STREET
DRUMMOND ST
Royal Museum
RICHMOND PLACE
PLEASANCE
National Museum of Scotland
WEST PORT
OLD TOWN
NICHOLSON STREET
Holyrood Park
POTTERROW
LAURISTON PLACE
University
ST LEONARD'S
GEORGE SQUARE
LAURISTON GARDENS
CHALMERS STREET
SOUTH SIDE
BUCCLEUCH STREET
ST LEONARD'S STREET
MEADOW LANE
West Meadow Park
CLERK STREET
East Meadow Park
MELVILLE DRIVE
LUTTON PLACE
HOLYROOD PARK ROAD
Bruntsfield Links
A700
WARRENDER PARK TERRACE
MARCHMONT CRES
MELVILLE TERRACE
CAUSEWAYSIDE
ARGYLE PLACE
SCIENNES
A701
SALISBURY ROAD
WARRENDER PARK ROAD
SCIENNES ROAD

while New Town begins at the busy Princes Street. The 'villages' of Dean Village, Stockbridge and Inverleith are easily reached on foot from the New Town. It's almost impossible to get lost around the tourist areas of the city, but good landmarks to head for, should you become separated from friends or family, are the Scott Monument on Princes Street and the Tron Church (see page 71) on the Royal Mile.

GETTING AROUND

Walking is by far the best way to see Edinburgh, to take in the many views and soak up the atmosphere of this buzzing city. It's easily possible to walk from the Old to the New Town in less than 20 minutes. Leith and the waterfront are also compact areas, and can be accessed from the centre of Edinburgh easily on foot, or by bus. Numbers 1, 10, 11, 16, 22, 34, 35 and 36 all either pass through the heart of Leith or arrive eventually at the waterfront. Unfortunately, Leith has no railway station, although a multi-million-pound tram project will be up and running by 2011, which should revolutionise transport between Edinburgh city centre and the waterfront (there is as yet no underground system in Edinburgh).

Glass-sheltered bus stops are in abundance, and display a plan of the route each numbered bus will take. Selected stops on the route are also written on the front of the bus. Single-day bus passes are available, or you can pay for single fares (but you must have the exact change).

For more information on routes and other details, contact **Lothian Buses** (t (0131) 554 4494 w www.lothianbuses.com).

Black cabs are in plentiful supply on Edinburgh's streets and can be hailed from the pavement if their yellow 'For Hire' light is on. Most taxi drivers are friendly and helpful and love to talk about their city with tourists. Fares are metered and the cost is

The roof of the Victorian ticket hall at Waverley Station

shown on a light above the driver's windscreen. At the end of your journey pay the driver through the glass cavity between the driver's and passenger's compartment. It's customary to offer a tip (around 10 per cent), particularly if the cabbie has been particularly friendly and skilled at avoiding main-road traffic. The limit of passengers per taxi is five people.

There are also various companies that you can telephone to order a taxi from your location:

Central Taxis (0131) 229 2468 www.taxis-edinburgh.co.uk
City Cabs (0131) 228 1211 www.citycabs.co.uk
ComCab (0131) 272 8000 www.comcab-edinburgh.co.uk

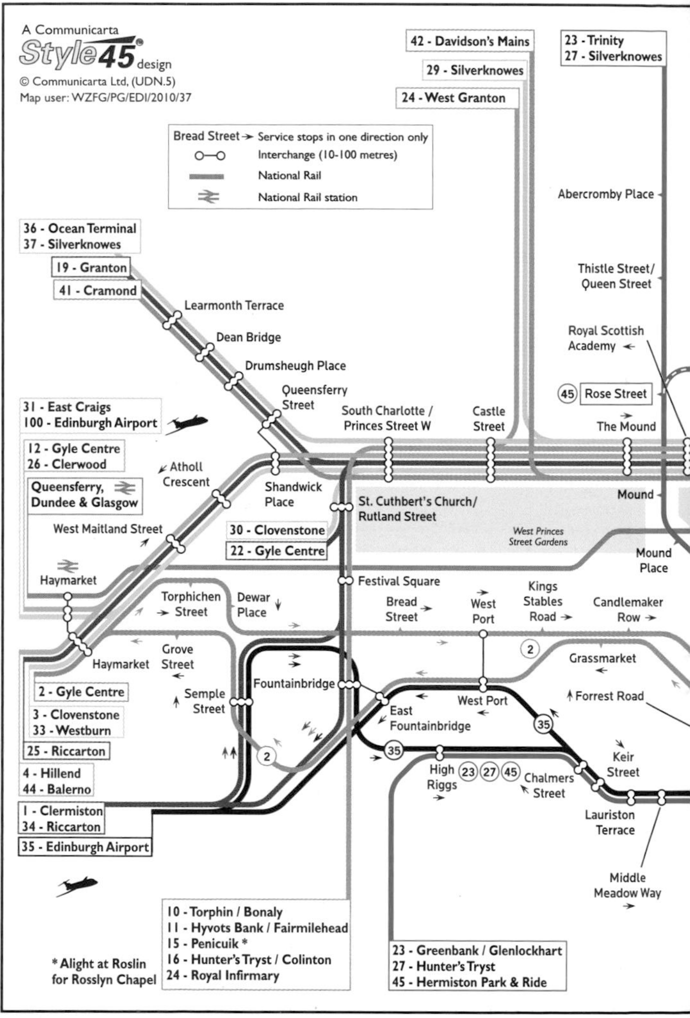

A Communicarta
Style45® design
© Communicarta Ltd, (UDN.5)
Map user: WZFG/PG/EDI/2010/37
Bread Street → Service stops in one direction only
Interchange (10-100 metres)
National Rail
National Rail station
42 - Davidson's Mains
29 - Silverknowes
24 - West Granton
23 - Trinity
27 - Silverknowes
Abercromby Place
Thistle Street/ Queen Street
Royal Scottish Academy
45 Rose Street
The Mound
36 - Ocean Terminal
37 - Silverknowes
19 - Granton
41 - Cramond
Learmonth Terrace
Dean Bridge
Drumsheugh Place
Queensferry Street
South Charlotte / Princes Street W
Castle Street
31 - East Craigs
100 - Edinburgh Airport
12 - Gyle Centre
26 - Clerwood
Queensferry, Dundee & Glasgow
Atholl Crescent
Shandwick Place
St. Cuthbert's Church/ Rutland Street
Mound
West Maitland Street
30 - Clovenstone
22 - Gyle Centre
West Princes Street Gardens
Mound Place
Haymarket
Festival Square
Torphichen Street
Dewar Place
Bread Street
West Port
Kings Stables Road
Candlemaker Row
2
Grassmarket
Haymarket
Grove Street
Fountainbridge
Semple Street
West Port
Forrest Road
2 - Gyle Centre
3 - Clovenstone
33 - Westburn
East Fountainbridge
35
25 - Riccarton
2
35
Keir Street
4 - Hillend
44 - Balerno
High Riggs
23 27 45
Chalmers Street
1 - Clermiston
34 - Riccarton
Lauriston Terrace
35 - Edinburgh Airport
Middle Meadow Way
10 - Torphin / Bonaly
11 - Hyvots Bank / Fairmilehead
15 - Penicuik *
16 - Hunter's Tryst / Colinton
24 - Royal Infirmary
* Alight at Roslin for Rosslyn Chapel
23 - Greenbank / Glenlockhart
27 - Hunter's Tryst
45 - Hermiston Park & Ride

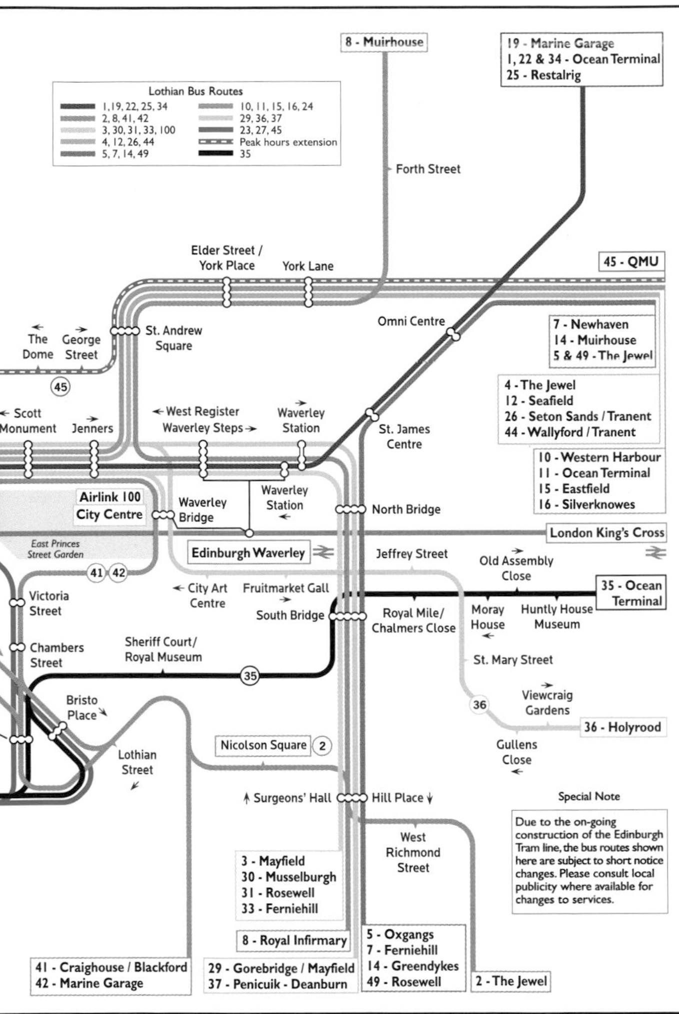
8 - Muirhouse
19 - Marine Garage
1, 22 & 34 - Ocean Terminal
25 - Restalrig
Lothian Bus Routes
1, 19, 22, 25, 34
2, 8, 41, 42
3, 30, 31, 33, 100
4, 12, 26, 44
5, 7, 14, 49
10, 11, 15, 16, 24
29, 36, 37
23, 27, 45
Peak hours extension
35
Forth Street
Elder Street / York Place
York Lane
45 - QMU
The Dome
George Street
St. Andrew Square
Omni Centre
7 - Newhaven
14 - Muirhouse
5 & 49 - The Jewel
4 - The Jewel
12 - Seafield
26 - Seton Sands / Tranent
44 - Wallyford / Tranent
Scott Monument
Jenners
West Register
Waverley Steps
Waverley Station
St. James Centre
10 - Western Harbour
11 - Ocean Terminal
15 - Eastfield
16 - Silverknowes
Airlink 100
City Centre
Waverley Bridge
Waverley Station
North Bridge
London King's Cross
East Princes Street Garden
Edinburgh Waverley
Jeffrey Street
Old Assembly Close
35 - Ocean Terminal
Victoria Street
City Art Centre
Fruitmarket Gall
South Bridge
Royal Mile/ Chalmers Close
Moray House
Huntly House Museum
Chambers Street
Sheriff Court/ Royal Museum
St. Mary Street
Bristo Place
Viewcraig Gardens
36 - Holyrood
Lothian Street
Nicolson Square
Gullens Close
Surgeons' Hall
Hill Place
West Richmond Street
3 - Mayfield
30 - Musselburgh
31 - Rosewell
33 - Ferniehill
8 - Royal Infirmary
5 - Oxgangs
7 - Ferniehill
14 - Greendykes
49 - Rosewell
41 - Craighouse / Blackford
42 - Marine Garage
29 - Gorebridge / Mayfield
37 - Penicuik - Deanburn
2 - The Jewel
Special Note
Due to the on-going construction of the Edinburgh Tram line, the bus routes shown here are subject to short notice changes. Please consult local publicity where available for changes to services.

Traffic can be heavy in Edinburgh and parking restrictions are rife so driving is not the most sensible option. If you do want to drive, however, make sure you understand the parking regulations, use pay-and-display ticket machines and never park on double yellow lines or red routes. Traffic wardens abound and are very keen on writing tickets.

If you're just coming into Edinburgh for the day, en route to other destinations, Lothian Buses (see page 56) operates a useful Park-and-Ride scheme, where you can park your car at two places outside the centre – Ingliston and Hermiston – then take a bus into the heart of the city.

Car hire

Hiring a car isn't necessary if you are only going to explore the city, but to reach the outlying areas, this can be a convenient way to get around. As well as multinational chains such as Avis (see below), there are several Edinburgh-based car-hire options. Costs obviously vary between companies, but the average cost for an economy-size car is £40 for a day and £150 for a week's hire.

Avis Wide range of cars, including people carriers, and one-way rentals are possible, dropping the car off at another Avis office. ⓐ 5 West Park Place (off Dalry Road), Haymarket ⓣ (0844) 544 6059 ⓦ www.avis.co.uk

Condor Self Drive Edinburgh's top car- and van-hire centre. Special weekend rates available and a free pick-up service. ⓐ 45 Lochrin Place, Tollcross ⓣ (0131) 229 6333 ⓦ www.condorselfdrive.co.uk

Thrifty Car Rental – Edinburgh Another multinational chain known for its good value. Drivers must be between 23 and 70 years of age. ⓐ 42 Haymarket Terrace ⓣ (0131) 337 1319 ⓦ www.thrifty.co.uk

Calton Hill with the City Observatory and monuments

THE CITY OF
Edinburgh

Old Town

Edinburgh has innumerable 'neighbourhoods' that can often change name from street to street, but its most clear divisions are between the Old Town and the New Town. It is the Old Town to which most tourists are drawn, for its medieval heritage, cobbled streets, haunted histories and the spectacular castle, all of which have earnt it a World Heritage Site status. One of this area's chief draws, the versatile Royal Museum, is undergoing major renovation and is closed until at least 2011, but, of course, the Old Town still has an embarrassment of historical and cultural riches with which to attract visitors.

The Royal Mile acts as a logical spine to the area, linking the castle with the wilderness that is Arthur's Seat (see page 70) and sprouting numerous interesting branches east and west of this renowned thoroughfare. The whole area is easily explored on foot, although the cobbles are unforgiving on high heels or unsturdy shoes.

SIGHTS & ATTRACTIONS

Dynamic Earth

One of Edinburgh's most unusual attractions, and perennially popular with children, is the large exhibition centre at the base of the Royal Mile, dedicated to exploring and understanding the planet Earth. From prehistoric landscapes to images of the earth's core, the exhibits also cover diverse climatic zones from tropical rainforest to Antarctic icebergs and volcanic regions. Various special exhibitions are held throughout the year, focusing on topics such as Scottish geology.
ⓐ Holyrood Road ⓣ (0131) 550 7800 ⓦ www.dynamicearth.co.uk

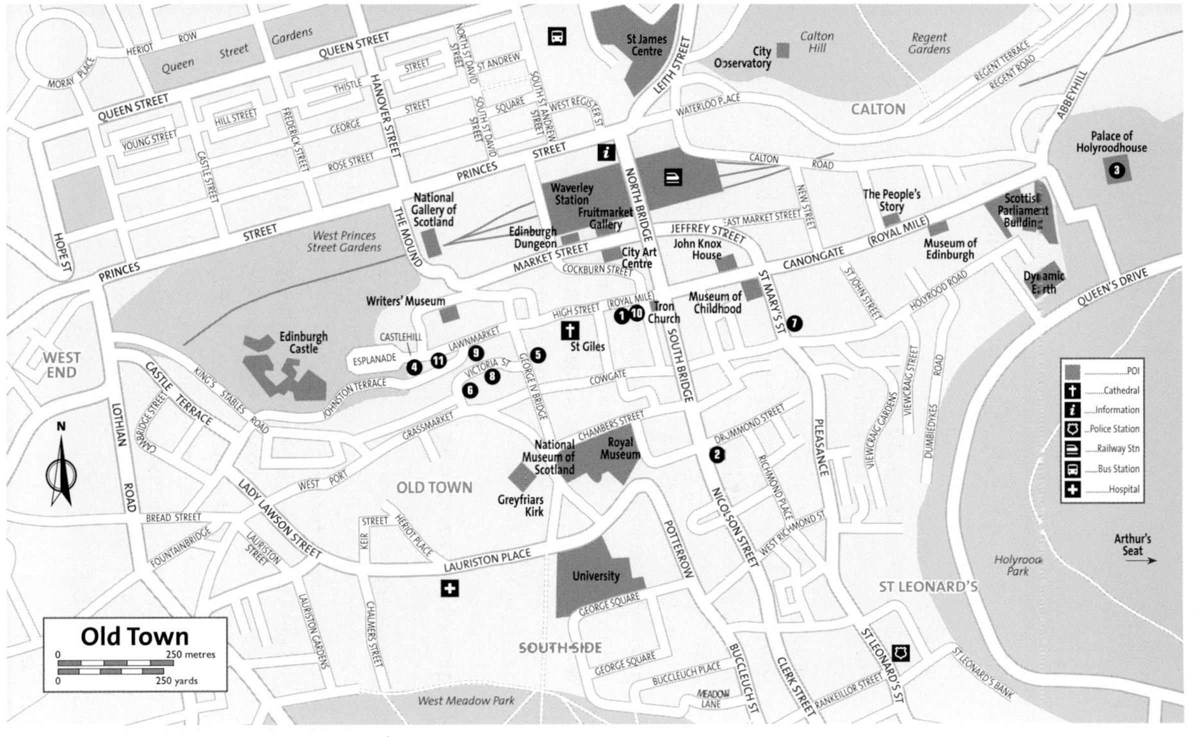

Old Town
0
250 metres
0
250 yards
N
POI
Cathedral
Information
Police Station
Railway Stn
Bus Station
Hospital
Palace of Holyroodhouse
Scottish Parliament Building
Dynamic Earth
Museum of Edinburgh
The People's Story
Museum of Childhood
John Knox House
Tron Church
City Art Centre
Fruitmarket Gallery
Waverley Station
Edinburgh Dungeon
St Giles
National Gallery of Scotland
Writers' Museum
Edinburgh Castle
National Museum of Scotland
Royal Museum
Greyfriars Kirk
University
City Observatory
St James Centre
Calton Hill
Regent Gardens
CALTON
West Princes Street Gardens
OLD TOWN
SOUTH SIDE
ST LEONARD'S
WEST END
Holyrood Park
Arthur's Seat
West Meadow Park
QUEEN STREET
Queen Street Gardens
HERIOT ROW
MORAY PLACE
HANOVER STREET
GEORGE STREET
ROSE STREET
PRINCES STREET
THISTLE STREET
HILL STREET
YOUNG STREET
CASTLE STREET
FREDERICK STREET
NORTH ST DAVID STREET
ST ANDREW SQUARE
SOUTH ST DAVID STREET
SOUTH ST ANDREW STREET
WEST REGISTER ST
LEITH STREET
WATERLOO PLACE
REGENT TERRACE
REGENT ROAD
ABBEYHILL
CALTON ROAD
NEW STREET
EAST MARKET STREET
JEFFREY STREET
CANONGATE
(ROYAL MILE)
NORTH BRIDGE
SOUTH BRIDGE
MARKET STREET
COCKBURN STREET
HIGH STREET
THE MOUND
CASTLEHILL
LAWNMARKET
ESPLANADE
JOHNSTON TERRACE
VICTORIA ST
GEORGE IV BRIDGE
COWGATE
CHAMBERS STREET
GRASSMARKET
KING'S STABLES ROAD
CASTLE TERRACE
CAMBRIDGE STREET
LOTHIAN ROAD
HOPE ST
BREAD STREET
FOUNTAINBRIDGE
LAURISTON STREET
LADY LAWSON STREET
WEST PORT
KEIR STREET
HERIOT PLACE
LAURISTON PLACE
LAURISTON GARDENS
CHALMERS STREET
GEORGE SQUARE
BUCCLEUCH PLACE
MEADOW LANE
BUCCLEUCH ST
POTTERROW
NICOLSON STREET
DRUMMOND STREET
RICHMOND PLACE
WEST RICHMOND ST
CLERK STREET
RANKEILLOR STREET
ST LEONARD'S ST
ST LEONARD'S BANK
PLEASANCE
ST MARY'S ST
ST JOHN STREET
HOLYROOD ROAD
VIEWCRAIG GARDENS
VIEWCRAIG STREET
DUMBIEDYKES ROAD
QUEEN'S DRIVE
1
2
3
4
5
6
7
8
9
10
11

10.00–17.30 (last admission 16.00) daily (Apr–June, Sept & Oct); 10.00–18.00 (last admission 16.30) daily (July & Aug); 10.00–17.30 (last admission 16.00) Wed–Sun (Nov–Mar) Admission charge

Edinburgh Castle

Perched high on a volcanic crag above the city, Edinburgh's castle is the capital's most famous and important sight. Home to the Scottish monarchy until the 17th century when James VI became James I of England, the castle has a long history of conflict between the English and the Scots. The oldest surviving part of the castle (and Edinburgh) today is St Margaret's Chapel, dating from the 12th century. Also on the site is the Scottish National War Memorial, erected to remember all the Scots who gave their lives in World War I, and subsequent conflicts. A tour of the interior of the castle gives a detailed view of the history of the Scottish monarchy, including the troubled journey of the Honours of the Kingdom (the Scottish Crown Jewels) culminating with a chance to look at this spectacular regalia behind heavily secured glass. Also in the castle is the Stone of Destiny (also known as the Stone of Scone). This square-shaped stone on which Scottish kings were traditionally crowned was stolen by King Edward I of England in 1296 and housed in Westminster Abbey, but was finally returned to Scotland, with much ceremony, in 1996. The Great Hall is also impressive for its vaulted ceiling and displays of historic weaponry and armour.

On the ramparts two cannons are popular attractions. The 15th-century Mons Meg is a siege gun presented to James II by the Duke of Burgundy, and the One O'Clock Gun is still fired every Monday to Saturday as a time signal. From here there are wonderful views across to the New Town, along Princes Street and up to Calton Hill.

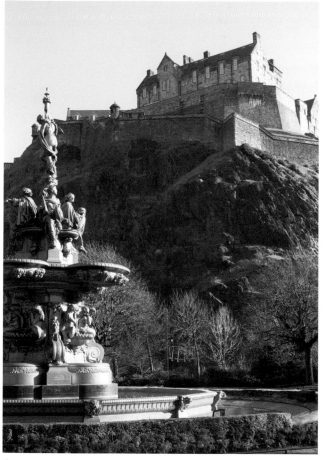

View of the castle from Princes Street Gardens

A statue commemorates the most loyal dog in the world

GREYFRIARS BOBBY

In 1858 an Edinburgh policeman by the name of John Gray passed away and was buried in Greyfriars Kirk. He left behind a devoted Skye terrier called Bobby, who pined for his master so much that he kept a vigil at his graveside for 14 years until he himself died at the age of 16. After unsuccessful attempts to remove the dog, the keeper of the churchyard gave him shelter and, in time, the sight of Bobby on his master's grave became the stuff of local legend. People would come specifically to see the dog, particularly at the time of the One O'Clock Gun (see page 64), when he would go to the same coffee house he had frequented with Gray and be given his midday meal. By 1867, when a law was passed requiring all dogs to be licensed, Bobby had become so famous that the Lord Provost of Edinburgh paid for his licence himself and the collar indicating this is now in the Museum of Edinburgh (see page 72).

In 1873, a year after Bobby died, a granite statue in his memory and in recognition of his devotion was erected opposite the churchyard, and can still be seen today, at the end of Chambers Street, in front of a pub also named in his honour. The story of Bobby has touched the hearts of many over the years, and has been turned into a feature film several times.

Also on the castle grounds is the **National War Museum of Scotland** (ⓣ (0131) 247 4413), where centuries of Scottish military activities are explored and illustrated with documents, uniforms and many other items. The castle is still a working military base, home to the Royal Scots Regiment, the Royal Scots Dragoon

Guards and Royal Military Police. ⓐ Castlehill, Royal Mile ⓣ (0131) 225 9846 ⓦ www.edinburghcastle.gov.uk ⓛ 09.30–18.00 daily (Apr–Sept); 09.30–17.00 daily (Oct–Mar) ⓘ Admission charge

Edinburgh Dungeon

A terrifying experience for children and adults, the dungeon – reported to be haunted – gives a fascinating insight into medieval Edinburgh, with realistic examples and displays of torture and brutal clan wars. The experience culminates with a boat ride through the sordid home of famous cannibal Sawney Bean. A terrific day out. ⓐ 31 Market Street ⓣ (0131) 240 1001 ⓦ www.thedungeons.com ⓛ 10.00–17.00 daily (Apr–June, Sept & Oct); 10.00–19.00 daily (July & Aug); 11.00–16.00 Mon–Fri, 10.00–17.00 Sat & Sun (Nov–Mar)

Greyfriars Kirk

This Old Town church is of great historical significance in Scotland as it was the first city church to be built after the Reformation and, more importantly, it was here that the National Covenant of 1638 was signed, marking the beginnings of the Presbyterian faith. Some 40 years later, in 1679, more than 1,000 Covenanters were imprisoned in the graveyard for three months, during which time many of them died from hunger. The area is now a museum and the Martyrs Monument commemorates those who perished. Many well-known names have their burial place here, including the architects John Adam and James Craig, and the poet Allan Ramsay. Many graves also still bear metal protective measures against the bodysnatching trend of the 19th century, in particular the notorious Burke and Hare. ⓐ Greyfriars Place ⓣ (0131) 225 1900 ⓛ 10.30–16.30 Mon–Fri, 10.30–14.30 Sat (Apr–Oct); 13.30–15.30 Thur (Nov–Mar); at other times by arrangement with the Visitors Officer

Palace of Holyroodhouse

Still the official royal residence in Scotland and a setting for state occasions, the Palace of Holyroodhouse was established as a monastery in 1128. After Edinburgh was declared the capital of Scotland in 1460 the abbey was converted into a palace by King James IV, moving the monarchy to this more attractive parkland and away from the castle. It is best known as the home of Mary, Queen of Scots (see page 122), who lived in the palace between 1561 and 1567, and it was also the

The Palace of Holyroodhouse remains an official royal residence

setting for the famous and mysterious murder of her private secretary David Rizzio by her husband Lord Darnley. Her private apartments have been preserved as they were in her day. The palace fell into decline during Cromwell's reign, but Charles II, who held his coronation here, oversaw many renovations including creating the Chapel Royal, and much of the Baroque detail dates from this time. In the 19th century further renovations were made when Queen Victoria returned to the tradition of using the palace as a royal residence when in Scotland. Ceremonial activities are largely carried out in the Great Gallery, lined with 89 portraits of Scottish kings by

ARTHUR'S SEAT

One of the most striking aspects of the city of Edinburgh is that it is sited on the landscape of extinct volcanoes, the most notable of these being the area known as Arthur's Seat, the looming mass that can be seen from many vantage points in the city. It's a popular spot for hikers, especially in summer, when views of Edinburgh, Fife and even the Highlands reward those who manage to reach the 251-m (823-ft) peak. It is also a chance to sample a piece of real Scottish wilderness without even having to leave the capital. Surrounding the peak is Holyrood Park, another popular day out for nature lovers in the heart of the city. The source of the name is unclear, but it is thought to relate to King Arthur, who was renowned as a legendary warrior among military outposts that were once located here. On the other side of the peak is Duddingston Village, an attractive enclave of Edinburgh boasting the country's oldest pub and a pretty bird-filled loch.

the artist Jacob de Wet, while each June and July the Queen holds a Holyrood Garden Party here. ⓐ Canongate, Royal Mile ⓣ (0131) 556 5100 ◷ 09.30–18.00 daily (Apr–Oct); 09.30–16.30 daily (Nov–Mar) ⓘ Admission charge; may be closed during official occasions, so phone ahead for details

Royal Mile

Officially called High Street, Lawnmarket, Canongate and Castlehill, the Royal Mile is thus nicknamed because of the route it takes between the castle and the Palace of Holyroodhouse. One of the most famous streets in Britain, its cobbled length throngs year-round with tourists, soaking up the atmosphere of tartan shops, the occasional bagpiping busker and a string of largely unimpressive cafés and restaurants. Starting from the castle end, the Tartan Weaving Mill (see page 51) and the Scotch Whisky Experience (see page 51) are well placed to trap tourists into buying two of the country's most enduring symbols. Nearby is Tolbooth Kirk, also known as 'The Hub' because it's where tickets for the Edinburgh Festival are sold, boasting the tallest spire in the city. Further down are Parliament Square and the **St Giles Cathedral** (ⓦ www.stgilescathedral.org.uk). On the pavement in front of Parliament Square is a heart-shaped stone known as the Heart of Midlothian, on the site of the former Tolbooth. Spitting on the stone is supposed to bring good luck and a promised return to the city, even if the superstition is a little uncouth. The High Kirk of Edinburgh, as St Giles is also called, was instrumental in the establishment of the Presbyterian Church of Scotland, but today is notable for its stained-glass windows and an ornate chapel added to the church in 1911. Almost opposite the church, beneath the City Chambers, is The Real Mary King's Close (see page 50). Further down, still on the same side of the road as St Giles, is the **Tron Church**

(ⓐ Junction of the Royal Mile and South Bridge), dating from 1637. Inside there are also views of excavations of the cellars that began in the 1970s and offer a fascinating insight into underground Edinburgh centuries ago. The church gets its name from the Tron, a public weighing machine for merchants, which was once sited here. Almost opposite the Museum of Childhood (see page 74) is **John Knox House** (ⓐ 43–45 High Street ⓣ (0131) 556 9579), a quirky 15th-century building that is now a museum dedicated to the life and work of Knox, the Calvinist leader and a great inspiration in the forming of the National Covenant and the Presbyterian Church. Two museums dedicated to local city life sit opposite each other on the area of the Mile known as Canongate. The **Museum of Edinburgh** (ⓐ 142 Canongate ⓣ (0131) 529 4143) has various displays recounting the history of the city, including the National Covenant of 1638, while **The People's Story** (ⓐ 163 Canongate ⓣ (0131) 529 4057) is a more evocative exhibition detailing the squalid and impoverished conditions endured by citizens in the 18th and 19th centuries. Rooms such as a prison cell, a wash house and a pub are re-created with historical detail while tales are told through oral observations from characters such as a fishwife, a servant and a merchant.

Scottish Parliament building

One of the most controversial buildings in modern Edinburgh history is the Scottish Parliament, designed by the Catalan architect Enric Miralles. There are many reasons for the debate: the choice of a foreign architect was unpopular; the cost of the building escalated far beyond the proposed budget, which many Edinburghers felt should have been spent elsewhere; and the futuristic design, including a roof that is supposed to reflect upturned fishing boats, was not felt to be in keeping with the rest of the Old Town landscape. It has, however,

The Scottish Parliament building

won many architectural awards since it opened in 2004, including the Stirling Prize in 2005. Although Scotland was governed by the Parliament in London for almost 300 years, there was a long push for devolution, and the Scottish Parliament was finally established in 1998. While matters of national importance are still governed by Westminster, the Scottish Parliament has limited power over domestic issues such as agriculture, health and some taxes, such as council tax. It also oversees the Scottish Executive, the Scottish branch of the civil service. ⓐ Canongate, Royal Mile ⓣ (0131) 348 5200 ⓦ www.scottish.parliament.uk ⓛ Visitor Centre 10.00–17.30 Mon & Fri, 11.00–17.30 Sat, closed Sun (Apr–Sept); 10.00–16.00 Mon & Fri, 09.00–18.30 Tues–Thur, 11.00–17.30 Sat, closed Sun (Oct–Mar), when Parliament is sitting

CULTURE

City Art Centre

The City Art Centre is best known for its regularly changing temporary exhibitions, which have covered themes as diverse as Egyptology and *Star Trek*. Within its permanent collection are some of the city's finest Scottish works, including the Scottish Colourists, sculpture and photography. There is also a café and shop. ⓐ 2 Market Street ⓣ (0131) 529 3993 ⓦ www.edinburghmuseums.org.uk ◷ 10.00–17.00 Mon–Sat, 12.00–17.00 Sun ⓘ Admission charge for temporary exhibitions

Fruitmarket Gallery

If conceptual art is your thing, including art installations, large-scale sculpture, videos and all manner of the weird and the wonderful, then you're likely to enjoy whatever current exhibit is on at the Fruitmarket Gallery. There's also an excellent art bookshop here, and a lovely café. ⓐ 45 Market Street ⓣ (0131) 225 2383 ⓦ http://fruitmarket.co.uk ◷ 11.00–18.00 Mon–Sat, 12.00–17.00 Sun

Museum of Childhood

As much a nostalgic treat for adults as it is a fascinating step back in time for children, different areas of this eclectic museum gather together toys from days gone by, including a doll gallery, train sets, board games and penny arcades. There's also a set of historic dioramas, including a pre-war schoolroom and a Victorian parlour, as well as many interactive opportunities on each level, such as a puppet show and a dressing-up box. ⓐ 42 High Street, Royal Mile ⓣ (0131) 529 4142 ⓦ www.edinburghmuseums.org.uk ◷ 10.00–17.00 Mon–Sat, 12.00–17.00 Sun

National Museum of Scotland

The National Museum of Scotland traces the full history of the country from prehistoric times to the present day. Of particular interest are the areas exploring Gaelic Scotland, the Jacobite uprising led by Bonnie Prince Charlie, exploration into the production of tartan and paisley cloth, and the effects of the Industrial Revolution, including some original steam engines and a whisky distillery.
ⓐ Chambers Street ⓣ (0131) 225 7534 ⓦ www.nms.ac.uk
ⓛ 10.00–17.00 daily

Writers' Museum

Scotland has produced many well-known writers, but three stand out as world-class literary figures: Robert Burns, Sir Walter Scott and Robert Louis Stevenson. This museum, set in a lovely, turreted 17th-century house, focuses on their three individual careers and includes many of their personal items, including Burns' writing desk and Stevenson's riding boots. Regular temporary exhibitions also pay homage to other Scottish writers of note. Outside the museum is a courtyard bearing quotations by a variety of Scottish authors.
ⓐ Lady Stair's Close (just off The Mound) ⓣ (0131) 529 4901
ⓦ www.edinburghmuseums.org.uk ⓛ 10.00–17.00 Mon–Sat, 12.00–17.00 Sun

RETAIL THERAPY

The Royal Mile is the place to head for if you're after touristy souvenirs, including everything in tartan, from umbrellas to dressed-up teddy bears. Just off the Royal Mile, Cockburn Street is the heart of flamboyant shopping in Edinburgh, with tattoo parlours, and second-hand clothes and record stores.

The Cigar Box A treasure trove of Cuban cigars, Zippo lighters and other smoking paraphernalia ⓐ 361 High Street, Royal Mile ⓣ (0131) 225 3534 ◷ 10.00–18.00 Mon–Sat, 12.30–18.00 Sun

Geoffrey Kiltmakers You can get your own kilt made up in your choice of tartan, as well as find numerous accessories associated with Highland dress. ⓐ 57–59 High Street, Royal Mile ⓣ (0131) 557 0256 ⓦ www.geoffreykilts.co.uk ◷ 09.00–17.30 Mon–Wed, Fri & Sat, 09.00–19.00 Thur, 11.00–17.00 Sun

Mr Wood's Fossils One of Edinburgh's most unusual shops, this specialises in fossils and minerals from around the world. ⓐ 5 Cowgatehead, Grassmarket ⓣ (0131) 220 1344 ⓦ www.mrwoods fossils.co.uk ◷ 10.00–17.30 daily (July, Aug & Dec); 10.00–17.30 Mon–Sat, closed Sun (Jan–June & Sept–Nov)

Royal Mile Whiskies A shop offering more than 1,000 malt whiskies, which make welcome gifts for friends back home. ⓐ 379–381 High Street, Royal Mile ⓣ (0131) 524 9380 ⓦ www.royalmilewhiskies.com ◷ 10.00–18.00 Mon–Sat, 12.30–20.00 Sun

Scottish Power Edinburgh Farmers' Market Every Saturday, farmers from all over Scotland gather to sell such produce as venison, wild boar, fish and seafood, as well as cheeses, chutneys and oatcakes. ⓐ Castle Terrace ⓣ (0131) 652 5940 ⓦ www.scottishfarmers markets.co.uk ◷ 09.00–14.00 Sat

The Tappit Hen Good-quality Scottish jewellery, particularly Celtic designs. ⓐ 89 High Street, Royal Mile ⓣ (0131) 557 1852 ⓦ www.jewellery-scottish.com ◷ 10.00–17.00 Mon–Sat, closed Sun

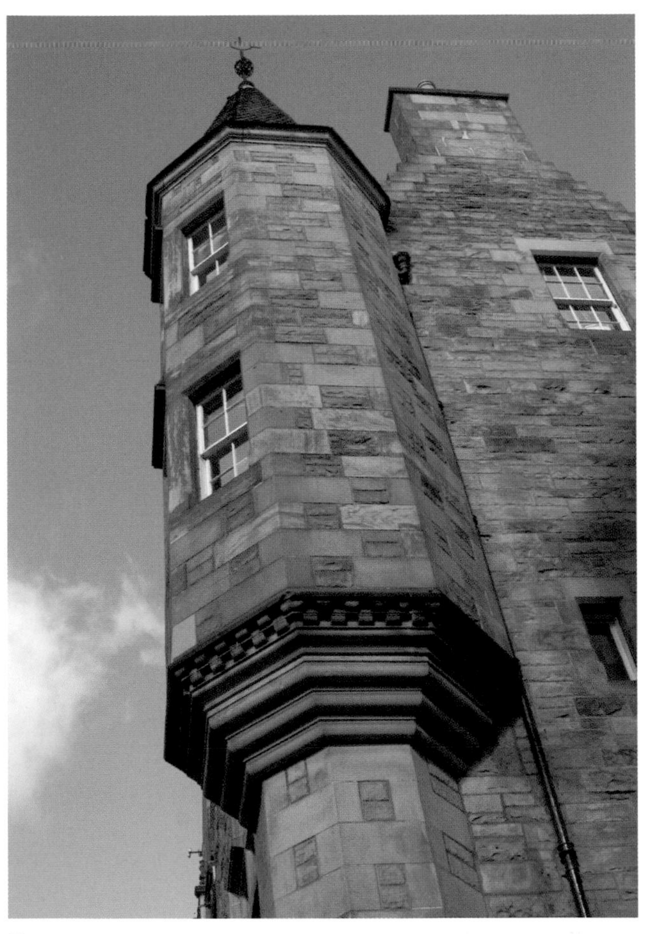

Spires like these are typical of the Royal Mile

TAKING A BREAK

Always Sunday £ ❶ A popular café, serving breakfasts, cakes, lunchtime snacks, fruit smoothies and fair-trade coffee. ⓐ 170 High Street, Royal Mile ⓣ (0131) 622 0667 ⓦ www.alwayssunday.co.uk ◷ 08.00–18.00 Mon–Fri, 09.00–18.00 Sat & Sun

Black Medicine Coffee Company £ ❷ An Italian coffee shop serving delicious cakes and panini, as well as, of course, top-quality Italian espressos and cappuccinos. ⓐ 2 Drummond Street ⓣ (0131) 557 6269 ◷ 08.00–20.00 Mon–Sat, 09.00–20.00 Sun

Café At The Palace £ ❸ Conveniently located for a visit to the Palace of Holyroodhouse, this lovely café serves hot and cold drinks and light snacks during the opening hours of the palace (see page 69). ⓐ Palace of Holyroodhouse, Canongate, Royal Mile ⓣ (0131) 652 3685 ◷ 09.00–18.00 daily

Cafe Hub £ ❹ Evocatively set within a renovated part of the Tolbooth Kirk, this is an ideal brunch setting near the castle. ⓐ Castlehill, Royal Mile ⓣ (0131) 473 2015 ⓦ www.thehub-edinburgh.com ◷ 10.00–23.00 daily

Elephant House £ ❺ A perennially popular snack stop, serving a variety of coffees and snacks such as bagels and sandwiches. More than 600 miniature elephants decorate the crowded location. ⓐ 21 George IV Bridge ⓣ (0131) 220 5355 ◷ 08.00–22.00 daily

Oink £ ❻ As its name suggests, pork is the order of the day here. A roasting pig is on display in the window, and pork sandwiches with or without apple sauce, freshly carved and served, make up the majority of the menu of this idiosyncratic café. ⓐ 34 Victoria Street ⓣ (0131) 220 0089 ◷ 11.00–19.00 daily

AFTER DARK

RESTAURANTS

David Bann Vegetarian Restaurant £ ❼ A top choice for vegetarians in the city with dishes such as walnut, hazelnut and mushroom haggis. ⓐ 56–58 St Mary's Street ⓣ (0131) 556 5888 ⓦ www.davidbann.com ◷ 11.00–01.00 daily

Khushi's ££ ❽ Entering the restaurant is like walking into a palace, and the two floors and hanging chandeliers just add to that feeling. The food is phenomenal and the waiters keen to strike a rapport with all customers straight away. Make sure you take your own alcohol, though, as it isn't licensed. ⓐ 9 Victoria Street ⓣ (0131) 220 0057 ⓦ www.khushis.com ◷ 12.00–15.00, 19.00–23.00 Mon–Sat, 12.00–15.00, 19.00–22.00 Sun

Maxies Bistro ££ ❾ Probably the most unusually set restaurant in the Old Town (it's poised on a terrace looking over Victoria Street). The inside is pleasant, and the menu caters well for vegetarians, seafood lovers and those with a hunger for stir-fry. The wine list is also fantastic. ⓐ 5B Johnston Terrace ⓣ (0131) 226 7770 ◷ 11.30–15.30, 19.00–23.00 daily

The Wee Windaes ££ ❿ This Scottish-themed restaurant boasts one of the finest views in the capital, looking up and down the Royal Mile. A wide-ranging menu, including the best haggis you can get in Edinburgh, is matched by an interior with a Victorian feel. ⓐ 144 High Street, Royal Mile ⓣ (0131) 225 5144 ⓦ www.weewindaes.co.uk ⓛ 12.00–14.30, 18.00–22.00 Tues–Sun, closed Mon

The Witchery by the Castle ££ ⓫ Considered by many to be the best restaurant in Scotland, this dark, atmospheric place near the entrance to the castle offers such Scottish specialities as wild salmon, fillet of beef and oysters all served with style and imagination. A favourite celebrity hangout for both local and visiting luminaries. ⓐ 352 Castlehill, Royal Mile ⓣ (0131) 225 5613 ⓦ www.thewitchery.com ⓛ 12.00–16.00, 17.30–23.30 daily

Enjoy a Scotch whisky in one of the many pubs in the Old Town

PUBS & BARS

The Albanach Conveniently situated on the Royal Mile, this is a lovely bar and restaurant that stocks more than 100 whiskies. ⓐ 197 High Street, Royal Mile ⓣ (0131) 220 5277 ◷ 10.00–01.00 daily

The Mitre This historic pub has all the comfort and advantages of a modern bar while maintaining historic features. ⓐ 133 High Street, Royal Mile ⓣ (0131) 524 0071 ◷ 11.00–23.00 daily

Sandy Bells This tiny, rather drab bar has earnt itself an international reputation for its nightly live folk music, largely provided by students under the guidance of friendly fiddler Freddie. ⓐ 25 Forrest Road (off Lauriston Place) ⓣ (0131) 225 2571 ◷ 11.00–24.00 daily

LIVE MUSIC & CLUBS

Dropkick Murphy's The huge room, which combines late-night drinking and live music from swashbuckling bands, is tunnel-shaped and lies beneath the city streets. Affordable and highly enjoyable – there is not a club with a livelier atmosphere in the whole of the city. ⓐ 7 Merchant Street (just off Cowgate) ⓣ (0131) 225 2002 ◷ 18.00–01.00 daily

Subway Cowgate A lively club with an eclectic range of music from its DJs, from punk to dub music. ⓐ 69 Cowgate ⓣ (0131) 225 6766 ◷ 19.30–01.00 daily

Whistle Binkies An unassuming basement venue with live music. Entry is rarely more than £2 and a range of bands from across Scotland plays every night until 3am. ⓐ 4 South Bridge ⓣ (0131) 557 5114 ⓦ www.whistlebinkies.com ◷ 19.00–03.30 daily

New Town

Edinburgh's Old Town may be the main tourist draw for its historic sights, but it is the New Town that gives the city its much-deserved reputation for elegance. The word 'New' is a bit of a misnomer these days, as the area dates from the 18th century, but compared to the medieval alleys and lanes up by the castle, these wide avenues and curving circuses must have seemed very new indeed. Much of the New Town owes its Georgian splendour to the architect James Craig, who was commissioned to create homes for the city's wealthy. Although very few of these are private houses today, their external gracefulness has been preserved. Another architect, Robert Adam, also made an impression on this part of the city with the design of areas such as Charlotte Square. Today, the New Town is considered the hub of Edinburgh, where most of the fashionable bars and restaurants are located, as well as designer shops, and there's a palpable sense of money in the air.

SIGHTS & ATTRACTIONS

Calton Hill

Edinburgh is often described as the 'Athens of the North', a term enhanced by its replica Parthenon looming down over the city from its position on Calton Hill. The folly is officially known as the National Monument, and was constructed by the architect Charles Cockerell in 1824 to commemorate those killed during the Napoleonic Wars. Also on the hill are Nelson's Monument, honouring the great admiral in the shape of a telescope, monuments to the national bard Robert Burns and to philosopher Dugald Stewart, and the City Observatory. Great views of the city

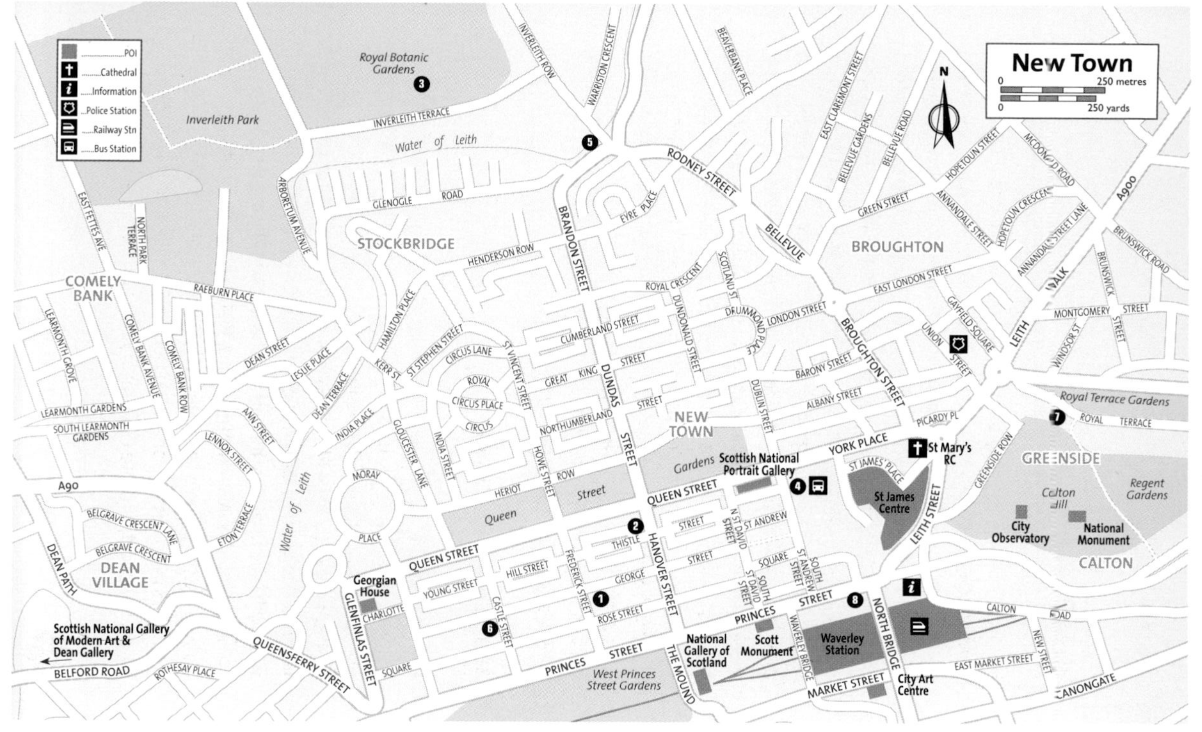

New Town
0
250 metres
0
250 yards
N
POI
Cathedral
Information
Police Station
Railway Stn
Bus Station
Royal Botanic Gardens
Inverleith Park
Water of Leith
STOCKBRIDGE
COMELY BANK
BROUGHTON
NEW TOWN
GREENSIDE
CALTON
DEAN VILLAGE
Royal Terrace Gardens
Regent Gardens
Calton Hill
City Observatory
National Monument
St Mary's RC
St James Centre
Scottish National Portrait Gallery
Georgian House
National Gallery of Scotland
Scott Monument
Waverley Station
City Art Centre
West Princes Street Gardens
Scottish National Gallery of Modern Art & Dean Gallery
Gardens
Queen Street
INVERLEITH ROW
WARRISTON CRESCENT
BEAVERBANK PLACE
EAST CLAREMONT STREET
BELLEVUE GARDENS
BELLEVUE ROAD
HOPETOUN STREET
MCDONALD ROAD
A900
INVERLEITH TERRACE
RODNEY STREET
BELLEVUE
GREEN STREET
ANNANDALE STREET
HOPETOUN CRESCENT
ANNANDALE STREET LANE
BRUNSWICK ROAD
BRUNSWICK STREET
EAST FETTES AVE
NORTH PARK TERRACE
ARBORETUM AVENUE
GLENOGLE ROAD
BRANDON STREET
EYRE PLACE
HENDERSON ROW
SCOTLAND ST
ROYAL CRESCENT
EAST LONDON STREET
LEITH WALK
MONTGOMERY STREET
WINDSOR ST
RAEBURN PLACE
HAMILTON PLACE
CUMBERLAND STREET
DUNDONALD STREET
DRUMMOND PLACE
LONDON STREET
BROUGHTON STREET
GAYFIELD SQUARE
UNION STREET
LEARMONTH GROVE
COMELY BANK AVENUE
COMELY BANK ROW
DEAN STREET
LESLIE PLACE
KERR ST
ST STEPHEN STREET
CIRCUS LANE
ST VINCENT STREET
GREAT KING STREET
DUNDAS STREET
BARONY STREET
ALBANY STREET
LEARMONTH GARDENS
SOUTH LEARMONTH GARDENS
ANN STREET
DEAN TERRACE
INDIA PLACE
ROYAL CIRCUS
CIRCUS PLACE
NORTHUMBERLAND STREET
DUBLIN STREET
PICARDY PL
ROYAL TERRACE
LENNOX STREET
GLOUCESTER LANE
INDIA STREET
HOWE STREET
HERIOT ROW
YORK PLACE
ST JAMES' PLACE
GREENSIDE ROW
A90
MORAY PLACE
QUEEN STREET
LEITH STREET
BELGRAVE CRESCENT LANE
BELGRAVE CRESCENT
ETON TERRACE
N ST DAVID STREET
ST ANDREW SQUARE
THISTLE STREET
HANOVER STREET
DEAN PATH
YOUNG STREET
HILL STREET
FREDERICK STREET
GEORGE STREET
SOUTH ST DAVID STREET
SOUTH ST ANDREW STREET
PRINCES STREET
NORTH BRIDGE
CALTON ROAD
CHARLOTTE SQUARE
CASTLE STREET
ROSE STREET
WAVERLEY BRIDGE
GLENFINLAS STREET
QUEENSFERRY STREET
BELFORD ROAD
ROTHESAY PLACE
THE MOUND
MARKET STREET
EAST MARKET STREET
NEW STREET
CANONGATE

can be had from the hilltop, but for even further-reaching views across to Fife, climb the telescope to take in the panorama.

Charlotte Square

This square is considered by many to be the *pièce de résistance* of the architect Robert Adam, who designed the square in the late 18th century. Today, it suffers somewhat from being a heavy traffic artery, but the quality of the architecture can still be seen. West Register House was originally a church, influenced by St Paul's Cathedral. At No 7 is the **Georgian House** (t (0844) 493 2118 w www.nts.org.uk 11.00–16.00 daily (1–28 Mar); 10.00–17.00 daily (29 Mar–end June & 30 Aug–end Oct); 10.00–18.00 daily (July–29 Aug); 11.00–15.00 daily (Nov)), built in 1796, and now preserved as a living example of the elegance of that age. Run by the National Trust for Scotland, various elements, such as paintings, furniture and silverware, are on display, giving a great insight into the lives of Edinburgh's aristocracy in Georgian times.

Dean Village

To the west of the New Town down in a valley off Queensferry Street is the charming and peaceful area known as Dean Village. Once a milling area that was separated from the city centre, it now makes for a pleasant stroll, particularly along the Water of Leith. Old mills and warehouses can still be seen, some of which have been turned into much-sought-after flats, and in all the atmosphere is quite at odds with the bustling capital just a few minutes away. Dean Village is also a must for art lovers, as it's the location for the Scottish National Gallery of Modern Art (see page 90) and the Dean Gallery (see page 89). Look out for six of Antony Gormley's naked figures at various points along the waterway.

Inverleith Park

One of the largest green spaces in Edinburgh, this beautifully situated park, in one of the city's wealthiest areas, boasts spectacular views straight through to the dominating Edinburgh skyline. Tree-lined paths and a sedate pond make you forget you are in a city at all. There are also spaces for football, cricket, rugby and bowls.
ⓐ Arboretum Place ⓣ (0131) 332 2368

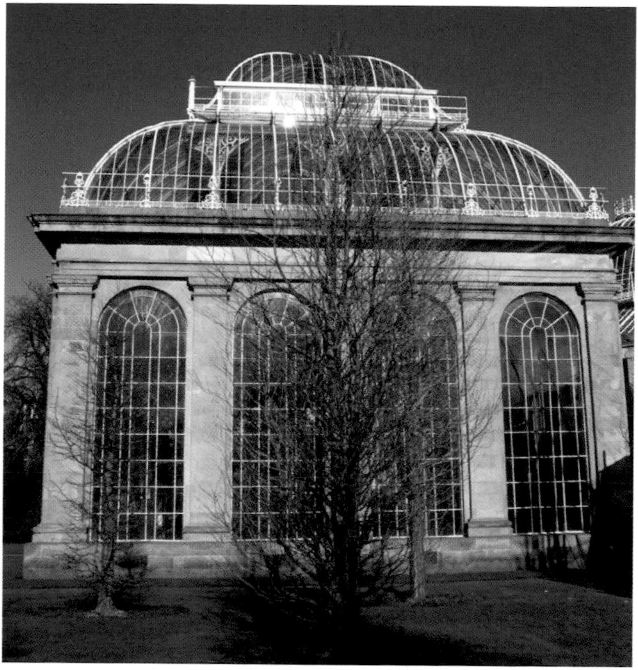

▲ *The tropical glasshouse in the Royal Botanic Gardens*

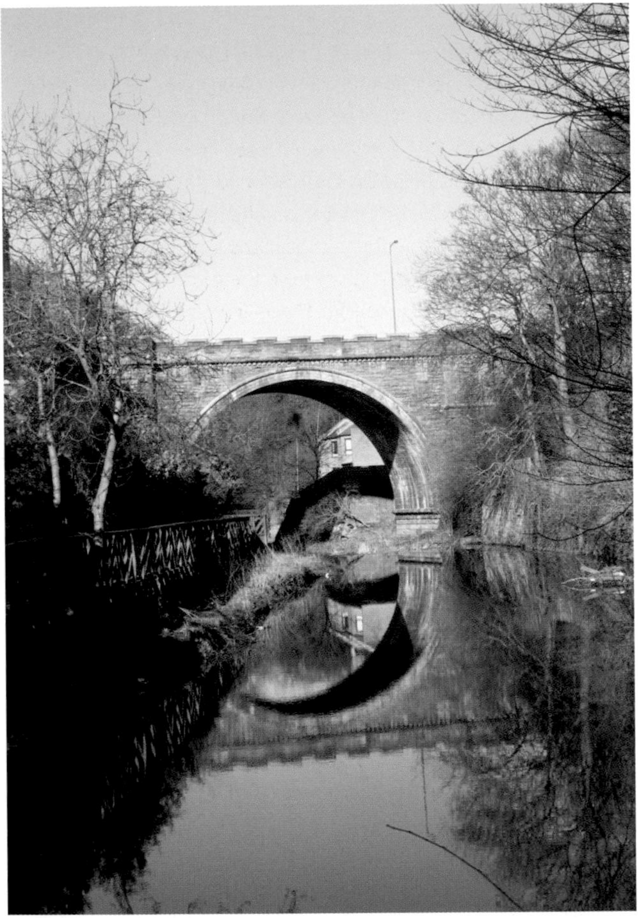

The Water of Leith is at its best in Stockbridge and Dean Village

Royal Botanic Gardens

Begun in the 17th century, these 30 hectares (74 acres) of land in the area of Inverleith are a stunning oasis of green in the city, particularly on a sunny spring day when the new flowers are coming into bloom. Although its main role is as a scientific research centre, it is nevertheless one of the city's major visitor attractions, with a rock garden, a Chinese garden, a tropical glasshouse, an orchid house, an aquatic house with rainforest specimens, and many other divided areas. The views of the city from the gardens' hilltops are some of the best in Edinburgh. ⓐ 20A Inverleith Row ⓣ (0131) 552 7171 ⓦ www.rbge.org.uk ◷ 10.00–18.00 daily (Mar & Oct); 10.00–19.00 daily (Apr–Sept); 10.00–16.00 daily (Nov–Feb) ⓘ Admission charge to enter the glasshouse

Stockbridge

A few minutes' walk from central New Town and you enter a whole new atmosphere in the village-like area of Stockbridge. Long known as the arty, bohemian side of the city, its main charm lies in its small art galleries, antiques shops, specialist food shops and smart wine bars and coffee shops. Slightly further along is Comely Bank, the setting for that great novel of Edinburgh snobbery *The Prime of Miss Jean Brodie*, while the fantastical building of **Fettes College** (ⓐ East Fettes Avenue ⓣ (0131) 332 2281 ⓦ www.fettes.com), which counts Tony Blair among its alumni, could well have been the inspiration for Harry Potter's Hogwarts school, with its baronial turrets and eerie style.

Water of Leith

The Water of Leith flows for 35 km (22 miles) from the Pentland Hills, outside the city, to the Leith waterfront, meandering through

the west of the city on its path. The most attractive part of the waterside is the path around Dean Village and Stockbridge, which is popular with cyclists, dog walkers and people just out for a stroll. The river was a vital source of industry in times

PRINCES STREET

When most people think of Edinburgh, the image that immediately comes to mind is bustling Princes Street and its spectacular view up to the castle and the Old Town, earning the capital the title 'City of Spires'. The street marks the division between the Old Town and the New Town, separated by bridges and the railway track that runs into Waverley Station. Although it is an extremely popular shopping street, the outlets here are standard to most British high streets and lack the exclusivity of areas such as George Street (see page 93). The main draw here, apart from the view, is the Princes Street Gardens. Formerly a city lake, the Nor' Loch, it was filled in during the 18th century when it had become overrun with sewage, and replaced by gardens, which are particularly attractive in winter when a Christmas market and funfair take place here. Near the station end of the street is the impressive Scott Monument, dedicated to the revered Scottish writer Sir Walter Scott. Designed in 1844 by George Kemp, a statue of Scott is framed by a number of characters from his novels beneath a 60-m (197-ft)-high Gothic arch. In the Princes Street Gardens West, don't miss the Floral Clock, the oldest of its kind in the world, replanted every year.

gone by when it helped drive waterwheels for the paper, flour and wool mills along its route, but this also meant that it was heavily polluted. Today, however, much wildlife, including trout and minnows, flourishes here.

CULTURE

Dean Gallery

While the Old Town is the part of the city to head for to discover excellent museums, the New Town is the home of Edinburgh's great art collections. One of the newer galleries is the Dean Gallery in Dean Village, opened in 1999 in a former hospital building specifically to house the work of the great Scottish sculptor Eduardo Paolozzi. It includes the huge robotic figure *Vulcan*, but is also home to an impressive Surrealist collection, including works by Salvador Dalí and Pablo Picasso. One of the most popular areas of the gallery is Paolozzi's re-created studio, filled with models, books and all manner of inspirational objects. The gallery also holds regular temporary exhibitions featuring specific artists or artistic schools, such as the Scottish colourists. There's also an excellent and very popular café within the building. ⓐ 73 Belford Road ⓣ (0131) 624 6200 ⓛ 10.00–19.00 Thur, 10.00–17.00 Fri–Wed

National Gallery of Scotland

For those with a more classic taste in art, this gallery, just off Princes Street, is the one to head for. Unlike many of its equivalents in other cities, it is of a very manageable size so you shouldn't experience art fatigue. The oldest gallery in Edinburgh, dating from 1859, it's home to a fine collection of Renaissance and Impressionist works, including masters such as Gauguin, Tiepolo, El Greco and Botticelli.

Furthermore, the gallery shouldn't be missed by anyone with a keen interest in Scottish art. Among its most famous paintings is the *Reverend Robert Walker Skating on Duddingston Loch* (1795) by Sir Henry Raeburn, which has become something of a symbol of the city. Various temporary exhibitions are also staged throughout the year, including a display of Turner watercolours every January. ⓐ The Mound ⓣ (0131) 624 6200 ◔ 10.00–19.00 Thur, 10.00–17.00 Fri–Wed

Scottish National Gallery of Modern Art

Across the road from the Dean Gallery, with gardens landscaped by Charles Jencks and decorated with sculptures by such luminaries as Henry Moore and Barbara Hepworth, the Scottish National Gallery of Modern Art focuses on art from the late 19th century onwards. Among the works are those by René Matisse, Francis Bacon, Andy Warhol and Lucien Freud, but the most famed collection is that of Scottish artists such as Sir William Gillies and Joan Eardley. ⓐ 75 Belford Road ⓣ (0131) 624 6200 ◔ 10.00–17.00 daily

Scottish National Portrait Gallery

Unsurprisingly all the portraits in the Scottish National Portrait Gallery's permanent exhibition are of eminent Scots, although visiting temporary exhibitions carry a broader theme. Among those immortalised on canvas are Mary, Queen of Scots, Robert Burns and Sir Walter Scott and, more recently, Sean Connery and the football manager Sir Alex Ferguson. There are also sculptures here, a photography collection and a numismatic collection of coins. The gallery's building is a star in its own right – an impressive 19th-century neo-Gothic sandstone edifice on the outside, and decorated with beautiful murals depicting the history of Scotland on the inside. ⓐ 1 Queen Street ⓣ (0131) 624 6200 ◔ Closed for renovation

Paolozzi sculpture of Newton in the gardens of the Dean Gallery

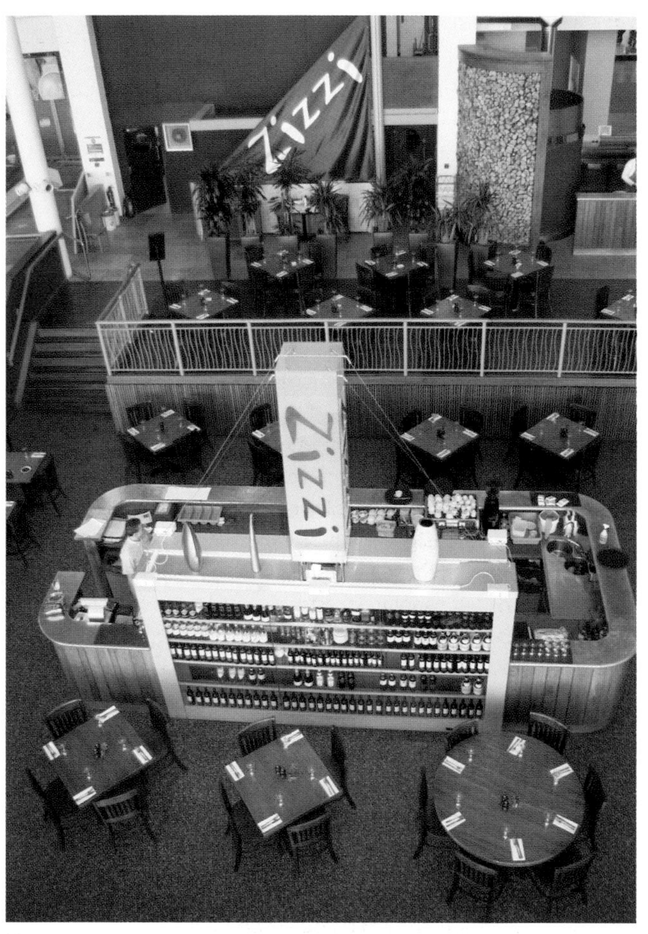

One of the smart contemporary restaurants in Ocean Terminal

RETAIL THERAPY

Princes Street is one of this area's two main shopping strips. Come here for the bustle and the views rather than the quality of the shopping, which is primarily made up of downmarket chains selling fashion, electrical goods and other paraphernalia that can be found on any high street in the country.

While Princes Street may be the most famous shopping street in Edinburgh, George Street, running parallel behind it, is certainly the most elegant. Not so much designer names but high-end fashion chains are to be found here. The street is lined with classy bars and coffee shops for when you're in need of refreshment.

Harvey Nichols One of London's most exclusive department stores opened its Edinburgh branch to much ceremony in 2002, and it is now the landmark of Multrees Walk, a pedestrianised walkway lined with designer names. Come here for a sense of luxury in toiletries, clothing and a superb food market, as well as an overpriced but panoramic restaurant on the fourth floor. ⓐ 30–34 St Andrew Square ⓣ (0131) 524 8388 ⓦ www.harveynichols.com ◷ 10.00–18.00 Mon–Wed, 10.00–20.00 Thur, 10.00–19.00 Fri & Sat, 11.00–18.00 Sun

Jenners Department Store Jenners is traditional in style, service and products, but popular nonetheless. It has occupied its prime Princes Street site since 1838. All the usual department store goods can be found here, but it's particularly strong on Scottish-produced items. ⓐ 48 Princes Street ⓣ (0844) 800 3725 ⓦ www.houseoffraser.co.uk ◷ 09.00–18.00 Mon–Sat, 11.00–18.00 Sun

St James Centre A convenient stop for everyday items and cheap fashion, with a branch of John Lewis. ⓐ Leith Street ⓣ (0131) 557 0050 ⓦ www.stjamesshopping.com ◷ 09.00–18.00 Mon–Wed, Fri & Sat, 09.00–20.00 Thur, 10.00–18.00 Sun

TAKING A BREAK

Café Rouge £ ❶ A take on a traditional Parisian bistro, this is a perennially popular spot, particularly on a sunny day when tables are laid out on the front terrace. Expect the usual French fare such as steak and frites. ⓐ 43 Frederick Street ⓣ (0131) 225 4515 ◷ 08.30–23.00 Mon–Sat, 08.30–22.30 Sun

Henderson's Salad Table £ ❷ A self-service vegetarian restaurant with a deli and takeaway facilities too. A great lunch choice, even if you're a committed carnivore. ⓐ 94 Hanover Street ⓣ (0131) 225 2131 ⓦ www.hendersonsofedinburgh.co.uk ◷ 08.00–19.00 Mon–Fri, 10.00–18.00 Sat; 11.00–16.00 Sun (Aug & Dec)

Terrace Café £ ❸ If you're visiting the Royal Botanic Gardens and it's a sunny day, don't miss the opportunity to soak up the warmth and the views from the lovely Terrace Café. Seating inside and out. ⓐ Inverleith Row ⓣ (0131) 552 0606 ◷ 10.00–17.15 daily (Mar & Oct); 10.00–18.15 daily (Apr–Sept); 10.00–15.15 daily (Nov–Feb)

VinCaffè £–££ ❹ An addition to Valvona & Crolla's flagship store on Leith Walk (see page 106), the VinCaffè does sell a small selection of the famous Italian produce, but it is mainly a café and restaurant. Downstairs are more informal sandwiches and snacks, while upstairs is a smart but reasonably priced restaurant serving excellent Italian cuisine. ⓐ 11 Multrees Walk (near St Andrew Square) ⓣ (0131) 557 0088 ⓛ 09.30–23.00 Mon–Sat, 12.00–17.00 Sun

AFTER DARK

RESTAURANTS

Loon Fung £–££ ❺ Considered by many to be the best Chinese restaurant in the city, this stalwart specialises in dim sum and a range of other Cantonese dishes. ⓐ 2 Warriston Place (off Inverleith Row) ⓣ (0131) 556 1781 ⓛ 12.00–23.00 Mon–Thur, 12.00–24.00 Fri, 14.00–24.00 Sat, 14.00–23.00 Sun

Oloroso ££ ❻ One of the city's finest restaurants and a celebrity favourite, with a stylish dining room combining classic white tablecloth elegance with a modern feel. The roof terrace has great views of the castle. The à la carte menu changes daily and there's also a grill menu. ⓐ 33 Castle Street ⓣ (0131) 226 7614 ⓦ www.oloroso.co.uk ⓛ 12.00–14.30, 19.00–22.30 daily

21212 £££ ❼ One of the newest and most acclaimed restaurants on the Edinburgh scene, Michelin-starred chef Paul Kitching has developed an intriguing menu. The setting is beautiful too, in a former town house on one of the city's most elegant streets. ⓐ 3 Royal Terrace ⓣ (0131) 523 1030 ⓛ 12.00–22.30 Tues–Sat, closed Sun & Mon

Number One £££ ❽ This Michelin-starred restaurant within The Balmoral hotel (see page 40) offers superb cuisine using the best of Scottish produce. Try the hare and rabbit terrine, or the guinea fowl. ⓐ 1 Princes Street ⓣ (0131) 557 6727 ⓛ 18.30–21.45 daily

PUBS & BARS

Barony Bar The Barony is known for its Victorian tiles and authentic atmosphere. It does get crowded, but for good reason, and there's a mixed crowd. Live music on Sundays. ⓐ 81–85 Broughton Street ⓣ (0131) 558 2874 ⓛ 10.30–23.30 Mon–Sat, 11.00–22.00 Sun

Hector's A stylish wine bar in the Stockbridge area, generally appealing to the younger end of the drinking market, but that's not to say it's rowdy, as it has a refined, arty kind of atmosphere. ⓐ 47–49 Deanhaugh Street (near Raeburn Place) ⓣ (0131) 343 1735 ⓛ 11.00–23.30 Mon–Sat, 11.00–22.30 Sun

The Oxford Bar They rarely come more traditional than this. Made famous by Ian Rankin's Rebus crime novels, as this was the watering hole of choice for the fictional inspector. Expect sparse décor, a collection of old cronies drinking and chatting at the tiny bar and creaky chairs

The Oxford Bar, the favourite pub of Ian Rankin's character Rebus

in a small upstairs back room. But then that's what gives it its appeal. ⓐ 8 Young Street ⓣ (0131) 539 7119 ⓦ www.oxfordbar.com ◷ 10.30–23.30 Mon–Fri, 11.00–01.30 Sat, 11.00–23.00 Sun

LIVE MUSIC & CLUBS

Fingers Piano Bar Pianists tinkle effortlessly away at the beautiful-sounding piano every night of the week. This classic bar is open until 3am without an entrance fee or thumping music and the obligation to dance. A real mainstay on the Edinburgh music circuit, and an incredibly relaxed atmosphere. ⓐ 61A Frederick Street ⓣ (0131) 225 3026 ◷ 11.30–01.00 Mon–Fri, 11.00–02.30 Sat, 11.00–23.00 Sun

The Jam House Jools Holland's live-music venue offers music every night, from mellow jazz and blues before 10pm to more lively music into the early hours. Food is also served. Over 21s only, and no trainers allowed. ⓐ 5 Queen Street ⓣ (0131) 226 4380 ⓦ www.thejamhouse.com ◷ 12.30–02.30 Mon–Sat, 12.00–23.00 Sun

Opal Lounge The premier venue for celebrity spotting, this is usually the final destination of the night for anyone from footballers to actors from all over the country. The trendiest club in Edinburgh, the Opal Lounge is now firmly established as somewhere for expensive champagne and glorious modern décor. ⓐ 51A George Street ⓣ (0131) 226 2275 ⓦ www.opallounge.co.uk ◷ 11.00–03.00 daily

Shanghai This nightclub is part of a wider complex, which also features bars named Vienna, Paris and Milan. They all come together under the Le Monde umbrella. It oozes class, and offers separate rooms for coffee, cocktails and wine. ⓐ 16 George Street ⓣ (0131) 270 3900 ⓦ www.lemondehotel.co.uk ◷ 12.00–03.00 daily

Leith & the waterfront

For many years Leith was the blot on Edinburgh's landscape – a rundown, working-class neighbourhood of abandoned docks that saw itself as apart from the rest of the city. Indeed, even today, Leithers are very proud of their individuality. In the 1980s, however, a regeneration programme was set in place and parts of Leith have since become some of the most fashionable parts of the city, particularly along The Shore area, where designer hotels and great pubs and restaurants line the waterfront. Do be careful in side streets after dark, however – it's not all rejuvenated just yet. It's easy to forget, when you're engrossed in the sights of the city centre, that Edinburgh is a coastal town, and further along are the lovely seaside 'villages' of Portobello and Musselburgh to the east and Newhaven to the west, which make ideal locations for a Sunday walk if the sun happens to come out.

SIGHTS & ATTRACTIONS

Commercial Quay

This former dock has now been converted into an atmospheric street complete with pond and fountain and lined with canopied restaurants. The entrance to the quay is marked by a sculpture of a fish and a boat to recall the city's fishing heritage. At weekends there is a covered market here selling antiques, second-hand clothes, books and more.

Leith Links

Although St Andrews often claims to be the birthplace of golf (as do several places in the area), it was at Leith Links, now a public park,

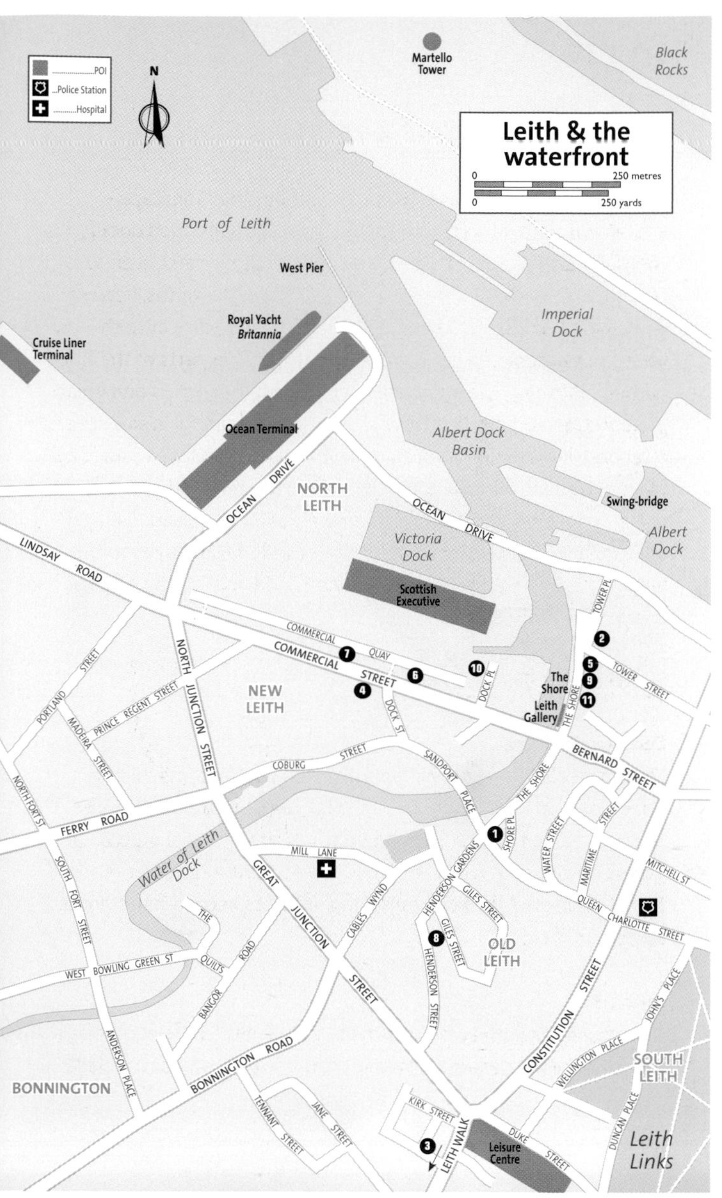

Leith & the waterfront
0 250 metres
0 250 yards
POI
Police Station
Hospital
N
Martello Tower
Black Rocks
Port of Leith
West Pier
Royal Yacht Britannia
Cruise Liner Terminal
Ocean Terminal
Imperial Dock
Albert Dock Basin
Swing-bridge
Albert Dock
NORTH LEITH
Victoria Dock
Scottish Executive
OCEAN DRIVE
LINDSAY ROAD
COMMERCIAL QUAY
COMMERCIAL STREET
NORTH JUNCTION STREET
NEW LEITH
DOCK PL
DOCK ST
TOWER PL
TOWER STREET
The Shore
Leith Gallery
THE SHORE
BERNARD STREET
PORTLAND STREET
MADEIRA STREET
PRINCE REGENT STREET
COBURG STREET
SANDPORT PLACE
NORTH FORT ST
FERRY ROAD
Water of Leith Dock
MILL LANE
SHORE PL
WATER STREET
MARITIME STREET
MITCHELL ST
GREAT JUNCTION STREET
CABLES WYND
HENDERSON GARDENS
GILES STREET
QUEEN CHARLOTTE STREET
SOUTH FORT STREET
THE QUILTS
ROAD
OLD LEITH
HENDERSON STREET
WEST BOWLING GREEN ST
BANGOR ROAD
CONSTITUTION STREET
JOHN'S PLACE
ANDERSON PLACE
BONNINGTON ROAD
WELLINGTON PLACE
SOUTH LEITH
BONNINGTON
TENNANT STREET
JANE STREET
KIRK STREET
LEITH WALK
DUNCAN PLACE
Leisure Centre
DUKE STREET
Leith Links
1
2
3
4
5
6
7
8
9
10
11

that the game was at least first recorded in the 15th century, and by the 18th century it was home to a five-hole course. The official rules of golf, which are still followed today, were settled here in 1744 by the Honourable Company of Edinburgh Golfers during the first-ever golfing competition.

Leith Walk

This long thoroughfare of bustling shops, pubs and Indian fast-food restaurants links the city centre with Leith, ending at what is known as the 'Foot o' the Walk'. There's not much by way of attractions on

A mural in Leith depicts the working-class roots of the area

this busy street, but it's interesting to take in the change of atmosphere between the top of the Walk and the foot, to see the clear distinction between Leith and the rest of the city. Near the city-centre end of the Walk, on Picardy Place, there's a statue of Sherlock Holmes to commemorate Arthur Conan Doyle's birthplace in a nearby house.

New Leith

New Leith is one of the most rapidly changing districts in Europe. The largest planning application ever to be submitted in Scotland

will, by 2015, have triggered the evolution of what was once a fishing town into a revolutionised, über-trendy district, with skyscrapers, offices and luxury flats, turning over a new Leith and giving the area a fresh Leith of life.

Old Leith

Old Leith has existed longer than Edinburgh itself. The port used to be a hive of industry and, although there has been a drastic decline in industrial activity, remnants from the old days are still evident on almost every corner (and the street layout is so intricate it resembles a maze). On various lampposts throughout Old Leith – traditionally stretching from Leith Walk down to The Shore – are attached green ears via which, if you call the advertised number, you get a story or legend about that particular area.

Portobello

Situated 8 km (5 miles) east of the city, Portobello is a slightly rundown seaside 'village' that was extremely popular with Edinburgh aristocracy in the 18th and 19th centuries. In summer it's usually crowded with families and dog walkers and makes a nice escape from the centre, with amusement arcades, ice-cream vendors and mini fair rides.

Royal Yacht *Britannia*

From 1953 to 1997 the Royal Yacht *Britannia* served the royal family on numerous trips and cruises around the world and is now permanently moored at Ocean Terminal. Apart from the restaurants and bars of the area, it's the main tourist draw for Leith and has done much to bolster the area's reputation. Inside, visitors can see the royal cabin-apartments, which are surprising in their homely feel,

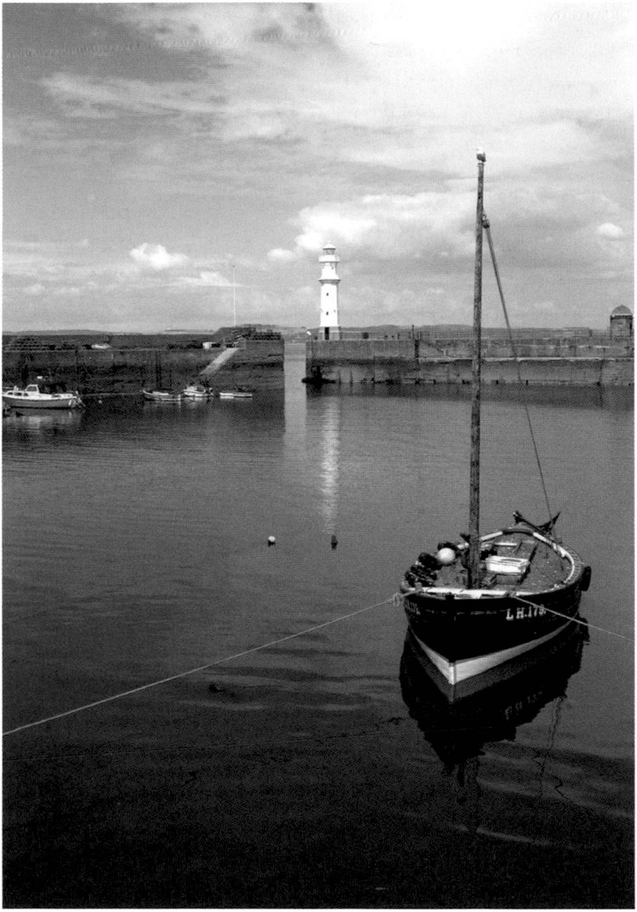

Newhaven lighthouse in Leith

filled with personal memorabilia and family mementos, and the great contrast of the grandeur of the state dining room. The yacht was also used for various royal honeymoons, including that of the Prince and Princess of Wales, who sailed around the Mediterranean for their trip. There's also plenty of information about the lives of the crew and their many duties, from the trivial to the arduous, and tours of the mess, the sick bay, the engine room and the bridge. ⓐ Ocean Terminal ⓣ (0131) 555 5566 ⓦ www.royalyachtbritannia.co.uk ⓛ 10.00–16.00 daily (Apr–June & Oct); 09.30–16.30 daily (July–Sept); 10.00–15.30 daily (Nov–Mar) ⓘ Admission charge

The Shore

The main focus of Leith's regeneration, The Shore is today a quaint area of restaurants, arty shops, luxury apartment blocks, and quirky sculpture that gives a nod to Edinburgh's seafaring past. It's particularly attractive on a sunny day when the many bars and cafés lay out pavement tables and you can enjoy a drink on the waterfront. Historically, this port area saw the export of coal and salt, while Baltic pine was imported here from Europe. Whaling was also handled from here from the 17th century.

CULTURE

Leith Gallery

This award-winning gallery is one of the best places in the city to see Scottish contemporary art, both established and up and coming. It stages a regularly changing programme of temporary exhibitions on all themes, including sculpture, ceramics and jewellery. ⓐ 65 The Shore ⓣ (0131) 553 5255 ⓦ www.the-leith-gallery.co.uk ⓛ 11.00–17.00 Mon–Fri, 11.00–16.00 Sat, closed Sun

TRAINSPOTTING

One of Scotland's most renowned modern-day writers is Irvine Welsh, who made his debut with the novel *Trainspotting* in 1993. Set largely in Leith in the 1980s, prior to its regeneration, it tells the tales of a group of heroin addicts in one of the worst drug enclaves in Britain. The stream-of-consciousness style, combined with the heavy use of Scots dialect, made for difficult reading for mainstream audiences, but the characters of Begbie, Sick Boy, Renton and others soon captured the public's imagination and it was nominated for the Booker Prize. The book was then translated into a play, and from that came a highly successful film, which made stars out of Scottish-born actors Ewan McGregor and Robert Carlyle. Many locations that feature in the film can still be visited. Tours of the area related to the book and the film can also be booked by phoning ⓣ (0131) 555 2500

RETAIL THERAPY

Diana Forrester An ideal place for gifts from around the world, particularly bath-time goodies and other luxury items for the home. ⓐ 54 Constitution Street ⓣ (0131) 554 4651 ⓦ www.dianaforrester.co.uk ⓛ 10.00–18.00 Mon–Sat, closed Sun

Flux Specialising in Scottish crafts but with plenty of other gift items too, including nicely designed cards, many of which are handmade. ⓐ 55 Bernard Street ⓣ (0131) 554 4075 ⓦ www.get2flux.co.uk ⓛ 10.00–18.00 Mon–Sat, 12.00–17.00 Sun

Ocean Terminal Designed by Sir Terence Conran, this is the smartest shopping centre in the city. More than 75 outlets make their home here. There's also a 12-screen cinema, a spa, an indoor skate park and some elegant restaurants on the first floor. ⓐ Ocean Drive ⓣ (0131) 555 8888 ⓦ www.oceanterminal.com ◷ 10.00–20.00 Mon–Fri, 10.00–19.00 Sat, 11.00–18.00 Sun

Relish A wonderful delicatessen not far from The Shore, with food and wine from all over the world and a superb collection of cheeses. There's also a small café at the front of the shop selling coffee and snacks. ⓐ 6 Commercial Street ⓣ (0131) 476 1920 ◷ 10.00–18.00 daily (Mar & Oct); 10.00–19.00 daily (Apr–Sept); 10.00–16.00 daily (Nov–Feb)

Valvona & Crolla First opened in 1934, this Italian deli has become an Edinburgh institution. Absolutely everything you could wish for in the way of Italian cuisine, including hams and salami, cheeses, superb olive oil, breads and wines, can be found here. There's also an on-site café-bar (see page 108), so you can sample the produce while you shop. ⓐ 19 Elm Row, Leith Walk ⓣ (0131) 556 6066 ⓦ www.valvonacrolla.co.uk ◷ 08.30–18.00 Mon–Thur, 08.00–18.30 Fri & Sat, 10.30–16.00 Sun

TAKING A BREAK

Café Truva £ ❶ Turkish meze, cakes, coffee and apple tea are all available from this specialist café. ⓐ 77 The Shore ⓣ (0131) 554 5502 ◷ 09.00–18.30 daily

Malmaison £ ❷ Whether you're after a light snack or just a drink, the bar of this well-known hotel (see page 39) makes for an elegant

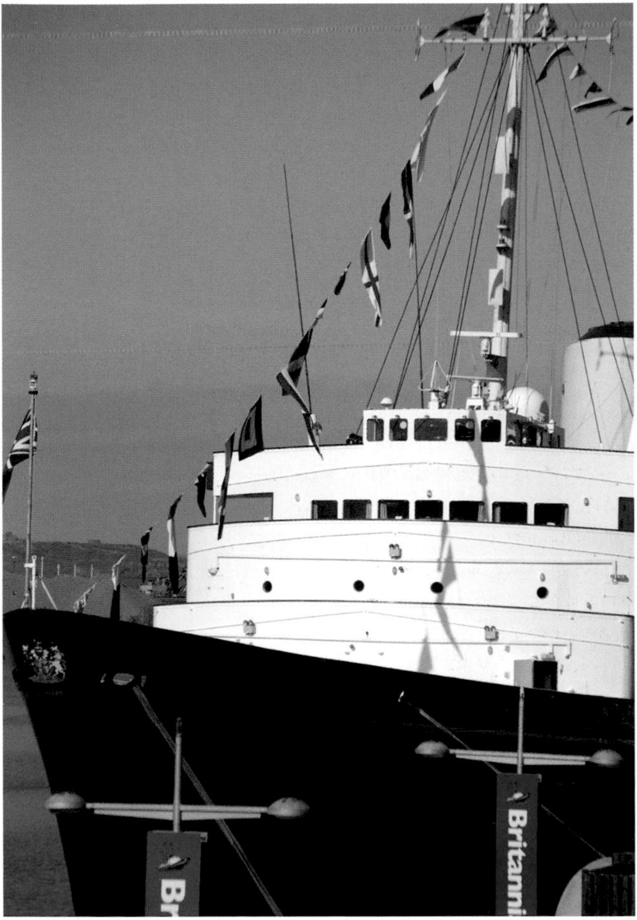

The royal yacht Britannia *can be visited at Ocean Terminal*

The Malmaison by night

refreshment stop. Enjoy an excellent glass of wine or a cocktail out on the terrace by Victoria Dock in sunny weather. 1 Tower Place (0131) 468 5000 09.00–01.00 Mon–Sat, 10.30–23.00 Sun (food served until 20.00)

Valvona & Crolla £ 3 For a mouthwatering bowl of spaghetti or a freshly baked pizza you can't go wrong with the Caffè Bar inside this famous deli's premises (see page 106).

AFTER DARK

RESTAURANTS

Daniel's Bistro £ ❹ A friendly, relaxed atmosphere and both French and Scottish cuisine make this a popular Leith hangout.
ⓐ 88 Commercial Street ⓣ (0131) 553 5933 ⓦ www.daniels-bistro.co.uk
🕒 12.00–15.00, 17.00–22.00 daily

Fishers £ ❺ Appropriately located near the waterfront, the fish and seafood restaurant is always crowded. Hearty fish soup, fresh

oysters and mussels are among the favourites. ⓐ 1 The Shore ⓣ (0131) 554 5666 ⓦ www.fishersbistros.co.uk ◷ 12.00–22.30 Mon–Sat, 12.30–22.30 Sun

International Starters £ ❻ A novel idea, serving a menu consisting entirely of starters, following cuisine from different parts of the world. The American menu includes fried chicken wings and Mexican tacos, while the Asian menu includes chicken satay and bhajis. ⓐ 82 Commercial Quay ⓣ (0131) 555 2546 ◷ 17.00–22.00 Mon–Fri, 12.00–22.00 Sat, 12.30–20.00 Sun

The Kitchin £–££ ❼ Owned by Tom Kitchin, the youngest ever Scottish chef to win a Michelin star, the restaurant prides itself on pure, fresh food that marries fresh, seasonal Scottish produce with French cooking techniques. ⓐ 78 Commercial Quay ⓣ (0131) 555 1755 ⓦ www.thekitchin.com ◷ 12.15–14.00, 18.30–22.00 Tues–Thur, 12.15–14.00, 18.30–22.30 Fri & Sat, closed Sun & Mon

The Raj £ ❽ Looking down on to the Water of Leith, this large circular restaurant is like a Victorian hotel dining room, with elevations and sprawling white tablecloths. The ambience created by the jovial waiters soon shakes any delusions of grandeur, and the Indian and Bangladeshi food is simply terrific. ⓐ 85–91 Henderson Street ⓣ (0131) 553 3980 ⓦ www.rajontheshore.com ◷ 12.00–14.30, 17.30–23.30 Sun–Thur, 12.00–14.30, 17.30–24.00 Fri & Sat

The Shore ££ ❾ The restaurant here specialises in local seafood in an elegant, wood-panelled dining room. There is a fixed-price menu for lunch on weekdays. ⓐ 3 The Shore ⓣ (0131) 553 5080 ⓦ www.theshore.biz ◷ 12.00–14.30, 18.00–22.30 daily

Skippers Seafood Bistro ££ ⑩ This is the best seafood restaurant in Leith, the menu changing daily according to the catch. ⓐ Dock Place ⓣ (0131) 554 1018 ◷ 12.00–14.30, 17.30–22.00 Mon & Wed–Fri, 12.00–15.30, 17.30–22.00 Sat, 12.00–14.30, 17.30–21.30 Sun, closed Tues

Restaurant Martin Wishart £££ ⑪ Another of Leith's Michelin-starred restaurants, this one serves a wonderful French-inspired menu of seafood, game and Scottish beef. Book well in advance. ⓐ 54 The Shore ⓣ (0131) 553 3557 ⓦ www.martin-wishart.co.uk ◷ 12.00–14.00, 19.00–22.00 Tues–Sat, closed Sun & Mon

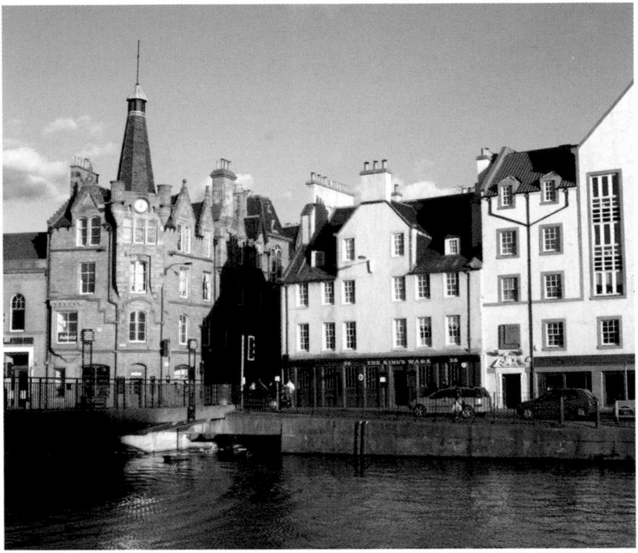

Restaurants line the attractive Shore in Leith

PUBS & BARS

Old Chain Pier A Newhaven favourite, this pub is built on an old sea wall and has spectacular views to Fife. The food offers standard pub fare such as steak and kidney pie and fish and chips, as well as local seafood, depending on the catch. ⓐ 32 Trinity Crescent (just off Lindsay Road) ⓣ (0131) 552 1233 ◷ 12.00–21.00 Mon–Sat, 12.30–20.00 Sun

The Ship on the Shore A cosy bar, all dark wood and velvet seating, that is also a popular restaurant in a bistro style. In summer it's popular for its outdoor tables looking right across the shore. ⓐ 24–26 The Shore ⓣ (0131) 555 0409 ⓦ www.theshipontheshore.co.uk ◷ 12.00–23.00 daily

Teuchters Landing All tartan and open fires, this is an ideal stop on a windy or rainy evening, while there is welcome outdoor space in summer. 'Teuchters' is the Scots word for people of Highland descent. ⓐ 1C Dock Place ⓣ (0131) 554 7437 ◷ 11.00–01.00 daily

The Waterline A laid-back, swanky bar is the last thing you would expect to find on this street corner, but The Waterline is ideal for a couple of afternoon beers or as the launch pad for a full-scale night out. ⓐ 58 The Shore ⓣ (0131) 554 2425 ◷ 11.00–24.00 daily

The River Tweed at Kelso

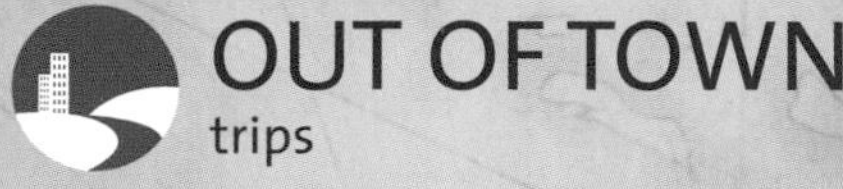
OUT OF TOWN
trips

The Firth of Forth

Temptingly close to the centre of Edinburgh, the coastline of the Firth of Forth and East Lothian beckons visitors with a range of purpose-made attractions, activities, historic sights and coastal landscapes. Portobello and Musselburgh are Edinburgh's own seaside suburbs, while the coast grows increasingly wild and windswept as you head east towards the North Sea. Long beaches and stretches of sand dunes and the gannet-haunted Bass Rock and other islands of the Forth estuary are on the horizon. This stretch of coastline has been the scene of many battles, from Roman times through to Cromwell's defeat of Montrose's Royalists at Dunbar to the last Jacobite victory at Prestonpans in 1745, and is studded with romantic ruins.

GETTING THERE

By rail

Frequent trains (at least one every hour) connect Edinburgh Waverley (see page 52) with Musselburgh, Prestonpans and North Berwick (a journey time of around 30 minutes), and Dunbar (around 45 minutes).

By road

Regional buses from Edinburgh's bus station near George Street take around 40 minutes to get to Gullane. If you're driving – which is by far the wisest option – the main A1 is the fast track to Haddington and Dunbar, while the A198 meanders along the coast through Prestonpans, Gullane and Dirleton to North Berwick.

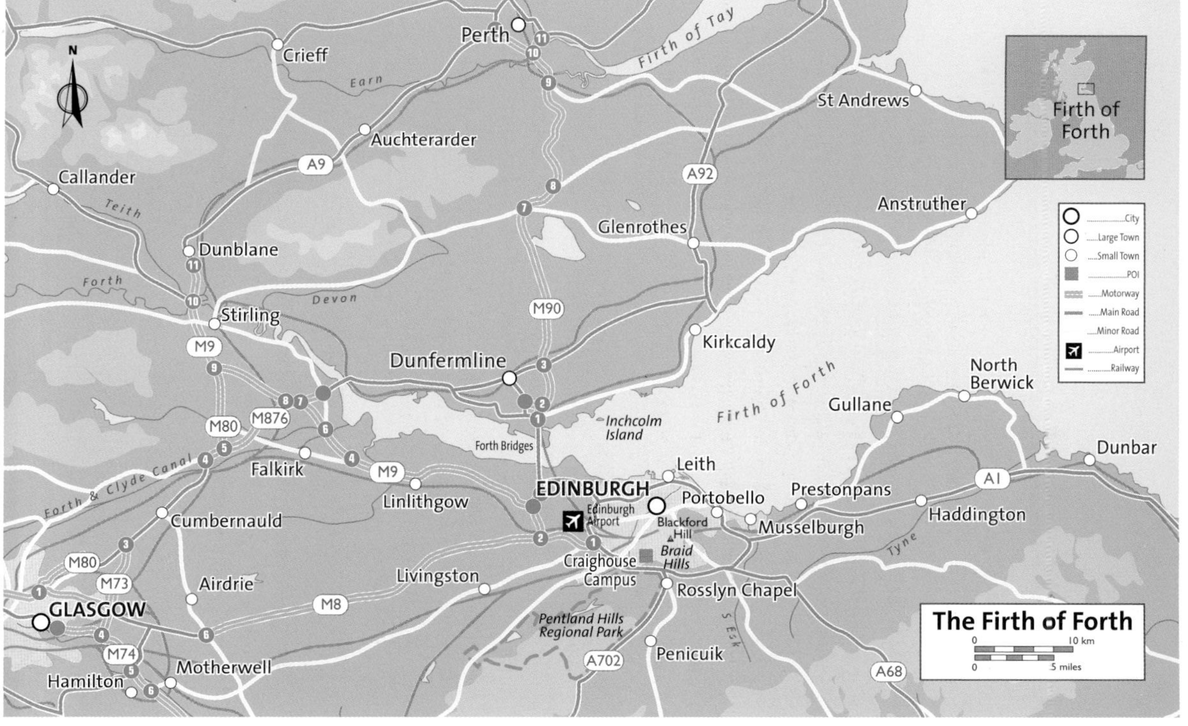

The Firth of Forth
0 10 km
0 5 miles
N
Firth of Forth
City
Large Town
Small Town
POI
Motorway
Main Road
Minor Road
Airport
Railway
Perth
Crieff
Earn
Firth of Tay
St Andrews
Auchterarder
A9
Callander
Teith
A92
Anstruther
Glenrothes
Dunblane
Forth
Devon
Stirling
M90
M9
Kirkcaldy
Dunfermline
North Berwick
Firth of Forth
Gullane
Inchcolm Island
M876
M80
Forth Bridges
Dunbar
Forth & Clyde Canal
Falkirk
Leith
EDINBURGH
A1
Linlithgow
Portobello
Prestonpans
Edinburgh Airport
Blackford Hill
Haddington
Musselburgh
Cumbernauld
Tyne
Braid Hills
Craighouse Campus
M73
Livingston
Airdrie
Rosslyn Chapel
GLASGOW
M8
Pentland Hills Regional Park
S Esk
M74
Penicuik
A702
A68
Motherwell
Hamilton

SIGHTS & ATTRACTIONS

Braid Hills/Blackford Hill

There can't be another one point in the UK where eight local authority areas are visible. But in the higher peaks of the Braid Hills, which adjoin the southwest and southeast of Edinburgh's outskirts, all four Lothian regions, as well as the Borders, Perth and Kinross, Fife and South Lanarkshire, can be seen. Three wonderful public golf courses are built into the hills, and at the nearby Blackford Hill – which takes all of 15 minutes to climb – the views are almost as spectacular.

Craighouse Campus

Undoubtedly Edinburgh's best-kept secret, this former asylum is now one of Napier University's many campuses. The views from both sides of the campus are stunning, and, despite belonging to the university, this is public land. From the front you can gaze back across the city and out to the North Sea, and from the back the Forth Bridges and Murrayfield can be seen. A nature trail winds through the campus and passes a pond and conservation zone. One of the finest free attractions in Scotland, and the architecture of the sandstone buildings is awe-inspiring. ⓐ Off Morningside Drive

Dunbar

Built of red sandstone that glows warmly when the sun shines, Dunbar was once a thriving North Sea port defended by a medieval castle. The castle is now a ruin, and the picturesque harbour is now home to more yachts and cruisers than fishing vessels, but Dunbar is still an attractive little town and a pleasant place to stop on a tour of the Lothian coast or the Borders, with some good hotels, restaurants and pubs. Just north of town, the sands and crags of

Lobster pots on Dunbar harbour

Belhaven Bay and the Tyne estuary form part of the John Muir Country Park, named after the Dunbar-born conservationist who founded one of the world's first national parks, Yosemite, after emigrating in the 19th century to California. You can visit his birthplace, on the High Street, and find out more about Dunbar's illustrious past at the neighbouring **Dunbar Museum** (ⓐ Town House, High Street, Dunbar ⓣ (01620) 828 204 ⓦ www.eastlothian.gov.uk/museums ❶ Closed for renovation).

Dunbar's famous **Belhaven Brewery** (ⓐ Spott Road Industrial Estate, Dunbar ⓣ (01368) 862 734 ⓦ www.belhaven.co.uk) can sadly no longer claim to be Scotland's oldest independent brewhouse following its takeover in 2005 by Greene King, but it still makes a fine pint and tours offer a rare chance to visit a working brewery – and taste its products.

Dunbar Tourist Information Centre ⓐ 143A High Street ⓣ (01368) 863 353 ⓦ www.dunbar.org.uk

Forth Bridges

Probably the most spectacular two bridges in Britain, the Forth Rail Bridge and the Forth Road Bridge straddle the watery expanse at parallel positions to each other. Prior to the rail bridge opening in 1890 a regular ferry plied the Forth between the Lothians and Fife, but the bridge considerably opened up the rest of Scotland to the rest of Britain. Fifty-seven men were killed during the construction of the cantilever crossing. Today, it is Scotland's largest listed construction. With the advent of heavier road traffic, it became clear in the 20th century that another bridge, for cars, was needed, and the Forth Road Bridge was opened in 1964, at the time the longest suspension bridge in Europe. It remains a toll bridge on the northbound route, still trying to recoup its more than £19 million construction costs.

The Forth Bridge connecting Edinburgh with Fife

Gullane

With its wild sweep of sandy beach and huge views out to sea, the stretch of coast between Yellowcraig and Gullane is the most breathtaking section of the Firth's south shore and the perfect place for a windy walk to sweep away the cobwebs of a night on Edinburgh's tiles.

Gullane's sandy dunes make superb golf courses, and nearby **Muirfield** (ⓣ (01620) 842 123) is renowned as one of Scotland's finest – despite the resolutely archaic, men-only rules of its governing body,

Beautiful Gullane beach

the Honourable Company of Edinburgh Golfers. While no pit of untrammelled licence itself, **Gullane Golf Club** (ⓐ West Links Road ⓣ (01620) 842 255 ⓦ www.gullanegolfclub.com) is rather more modern in outlook.

Inchcolm Island

This unusual island looks bleak and barren, but probably has one of the most spectacular situations in the world under both the Forth Road and Rail Bridges. Ferry services (ⓣ (0131) 331 5000 ⓦ www.maidoftheforth.co.uk) are available from the mainland to what is dubbed the 'Iona of the East', and on the boat across, seals (and possibly dolphins) will be visible.

Linlithgow

The picturesque town of Linlithgow is best known for **Linlithgow Palace** (ⓐ Kirkgate ⓣ (01506) 842 896), the birthplace of both James V and Mary, Queen of Scots, set on its own loch and in extensive parkland. Now partly a ruin, the great hall and chapel are still impressive. Also in Linlithgow is the 17th-century stately home known as the **House of the Binns** (ⓣ (01506) 834 255), once home to the Dalyells family. The house is filled with antiques and portraits, and is well worth a visit for anyone interested in the history of architecture.

North Berwick

North Berwick is a pretty town with a sweep of sandy beach that – before the advent of cheap package holidays to the Mediterranean – made it one of Scotland's premier seaside resorts. It's still a very attractive place for a day out. With several good hotels, restaurants and guesthouses, North Berwick is also a good base for an overnight stay

while exploring East Lothian. Just outside North Berwick, **Dirleton Castle** (ⓐ 5 km/3 miles west of North Berwick on the A198 ⓣ (01620) 850 330) is a romantic ruin set in traditional formal gardens and surrounded by what is claimed to be the world's longest herbaceous border – at least, according to *Guinness World Records*. The grimmer and more formidable-looking **Tantallon Castle** (ⓐ 4 km/2½ miles east of North Berwick on the A198 ⓣ (01620) 892 727) lies on a vertigo-

MARY, QUEEN OF SCOTS

Born in 1542, Mary became Queen of Scots when she was just six days old and she was a pawn in English and Scottish politics for the rest of her life. The Scots initially betrothed her to Henry VIII's son Edward in an attempt to unite the two countries. However, they then changed their mind in favour of France, sending her to the French royal court as the future wife of the Dauphin Francis at the age of six. She and the dauphin became King and Queen of France in 1558, but when the king died two years later, Mary returned to Scotland as monarch. It was her second marriage, however, to her cousin Lord Darnley that set the stage for her last tragic years; when he was murdered in 1567, many people questioned whether Mary or her third husband, the Earl of Bothwell, were responsible. By this time her Protestant subjects had grown tired of their Catholic queen and she was imprisoned at Lochleven Castle, abdicating the throne in favour of her young son James. In the hope that Elizabeth I would be an ally, she fled to England, where she was incarcerated for 19 years and finally executed in 1587 to put paid to the constant threat of Catholic ambitions.

Dirleton Castle was first built in the 13th century

The Bass Rock is a haven for seabirds

inducing cliff-top site at Tantallon. A stronghold of the Douglases – one of the great dynasties of medieval Scotland – Tantallon defied many sieges until the advent of artillery, and the era of peace with England, made it redundant, and it's now one of the region's most spectacular and evocative ruins.

In summer, North Berwick is the base for boat trips to the Bass Rock, a windswept, craggy islet about 1 km (½ mile) offshore, which guards the mouth of the Firth of Forth. Until the 18th century, this was an island fortress, defended by ramparts and batteries of cannon, and was also used as a prison for opponents of the Crown –

Scotland's equivalent of Alcatraz. Today, its fortifications demolished long ago, the 108-m (354-ft) crag is deserted except for huge flocks of nesting gannets, guillemots, puffins, razorbills, fulmars and kittiwakes. Those too timid to enjoy the boat trip can watch the birds live on the cameras of North Berwick's newest attraction, the **Scottish Seabird Centre** (ⓐ The Harbour, North Berwick ⓣ (01620) 890 202 ⓦ www.seabird.org), which show views of the Rock's seabird colonies and seal-breeding sites.

North Berwick Tourist Information Centre ⓐ 1 Quality Street ⓣ (0845) 22 55 121 ⓦ www.north-berwick.co.uk

Pentland Hills Regional Park

The hills that provide a shelter for the city play home to a few nice surprises. As well as stunning views and challenging hiking trails, there is a dry ski slope which is visible for miles around, golf courses and reservoirs. The Pentland Hills Regional Park also includes several

ACTIVITIES

Golf

The Forth coast claims to be the birthplace of golf. There are 19 top-quality courses around the East Lothian region – some of them legendary – and many are open to visiting golfers, while golf packages, including green fees, are available from most of Edinburgh's top hotels (most of which are only half an hour away) or from hotels catering to golf enthusiasts in and around Gullane and North Berwick. For information visit ⓦ www.golfeastlothian.com

Walking & cycling

East Lothian is the sunniest part of Scotland and great for walking. Hike up North Berwick Law or Traprain Law for great views across the border country and out to sea, or take a less energetic stroll along the John Muir Way from Musselburgh to Aberlady, or south from Dunbar. For cyclists there are three longer, waymarked trails from Musselburgh to Dunbar – the Forth Coastal Trail, the Hillfoots Trail through the foothills of the rolling Lammermuirs, and the Saltire Trail through the heart of East Lothian.

Wildlife

For birdwatchers, the Lothian countryside and the Forth coast are among the most exciting places in the British Isles. The Bass Rock (see page 124) is the home of one of the world's largest gannet colonies, and there are more accessible spots to see a range of waterfowl and other birds at Levenhall Links, at the mouth of the River Esk near Musselburgh, where tidal mudflats attract large numbers of gulls, ducks, geese and waders, and hides and shallow pools have been created to make viewing easy. Red deer and roe deer are sometimes seen in the Lammermuirs, and other wildlife in the region includes badgers, red squirrels and otters – making a comeback on waterways like the Esk and the Tyne.

For recommended companies offering wildlife-watching day trips and cruises on the Forth from Edinburgh and North Berwick, see the VisitScotland special wildlife site Ⓦ www.wild-scotland.co.uk

organised walks and conservation projects. ⓐ Biggar Road ⓣ (0131) 445 3383 ⓦ www.pentlandhills.org

TAKING A BREAK

The Lothian region has a wide choice of places to eat during the day and in the evening, ranging from basic pub food to lavish spreads in formal surroundings. Some of the best places to eat include:

Steading £ The last establishment you pass as you leave Edinburgh heading south is unmissable for one transfixing reason: haggis in batter. ⓐ 118 Biggar Road ⓣ (0131) 445 1128 ⓞ 10.00–23.00 Sun–Thur, 10.00–24.00 Fri & Sat

The Creel ££ This cosy restaurant near the old harbour serves excellent seafood. ⓐ 25 Lamer Street, The Old Harbour, Dunbar ⓣ (01368) 863 279 ⓦ www.creelrestaurant.co.uk ⓞ 12.00–14.00, 18.30–21.00 Thur–Sun, closed Mon–Wed

Morningside Spice ££ Considered by many to be the best Indian restaurant in the Lothians, this intimate restaurant offers its chef's brilliant chicken pasanda as the highlight of the numerous dishes. ⓐ 74 Morningside Road ⓣ (0131) 447 8787 ⓞ 12.00–15.00, 18.30–23.00 Mon–Thur, 12.00–15.00, 18.30–24.00 Fri & Sat, 19.00–22.30 Sun

ACCOMMODATION

For help with finding somewhere to stay, contact the Edinburgh and Scotland Information Centre (see page 153).

Borders & the Lothians

South of Edinburgh, within easy day-trip distance by bus or car, lies a patchwork of rich farming country dotted with small market towns and former mining villages, bordered by the rolling, grassy hills of the Southern Uplands – a region of moorland, sheep pastures, picturesque ruined abbeys, medieval castles and manor houses. Until the 18th century, the dales and hills of the Border country were an independent land, where local magnates took little notice of the royal powers of Edinburgh or London and where feuding and cattle raiding were a way of life, celebrated in the Border Ballads of Scotland's most famous author, Sir Walter Scott. Today, however, this is a far gentler landscape.

GETTING THERE

By road

The main A7 and A68 roads connect Edinburgh with Melrose (about one hour) and Jedburgh (about 90 minutes) and points south. There are frequent buses (at least six per day) from Edinburgh to Jedburgh, Melrose, Peebles and Galashiels, for details of which contact **Traveline** (t (0870) 608 2608 w www.traveline.org.uk).

SIGHTS & ATTRACTIONS

Jedburgh

Perilously close to the English border, this picturesque country town, with its castle and medieval abbey, bore the brunt of many invasions from across the River Tweed. Its eponymous castle was destroyed by

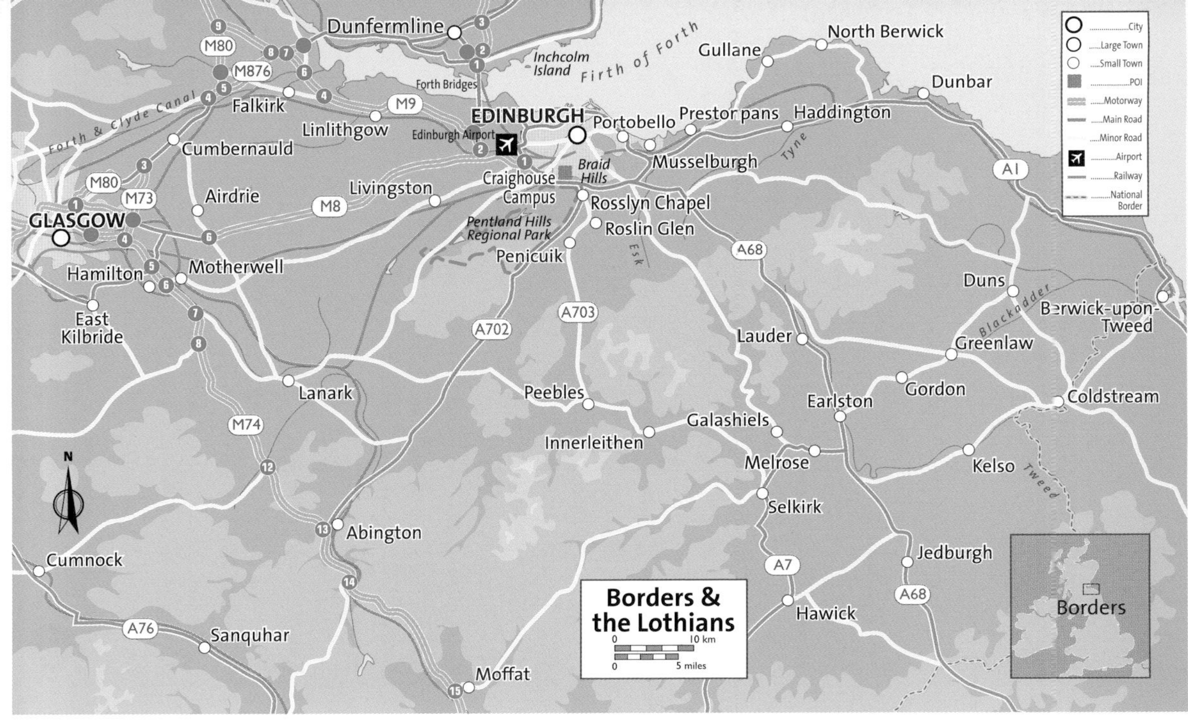
Borders &
the Lothians
0 10 km
0 5 miles
City
Large Town
Small Town
POI
Motorway
Main Road
Minor Road
Airport
Railway
National Border
Borders
N
Dunfermline
Firth of Forth
Inchcolm Island
Forth Bridges
North Berwick
Gullane
Dunbar
EDINBURGH
Edinburgh Airport
Portobello
Prestor pans
Haddington
Musselburgh
Tyne
Braid Hills
Craighouse Campus
Rosslyn Chapel
Roslin Glen
Pentland Hills Regional Park
Penicuik
Esk
Falkirk
Linlithgow
Forth & Clyde Canal
Cumbernauld
Airdrie
Livingston
GLASGOW
Motherwell
Hamilton
East Kilbride
Lanark
Peebles
Innerleithen
Galashiels
Melrose
Selkirk
Earlston
Lauder
Gordon
Greenlaw
Duns
Blackadder
Berwick-upon-Tweed
Coldstream
Kelso
Tweed
Jedburgh
Hawick
Abington
Moffat
Cumnock
Sanquhar
M80
M876
M9
M73
M8
A1
A68
A703
A702
M74
A7
A76

an English army in 1409, and **Jedburgh Abbey** (ⓐ 4 Abbey Bridge End ⓣ (01835) 863 925), which was once one of the wealthiest religious foundations in Scotland, was sacked during Henry VIII's Rough Wooing of Scotland in 1544 (when Henry sought to bully the Scots into marrying the infant Queen Mary to his son) and was finally abandoned after the Protestant Reformation. Founded in the 12th century during the reign of the pious King David I (who also founded the Abbey of Holyrood in Edinburgh), the abbey ranks – alongside **Hopetoun House** (ⓐ South Queensferry ⓣ (0131) 331 2451) – among Scotland's most picturesque sights, with a stone tower, fine stone carvings and a striking Catherine window. An excellent video illustrates the abbey's turbulent history. Scotland's ill-fated queen is said to have stayed at the house now known as **Mary, Queen of Scots House** (ⓐ Queen Street ⓣ (01835) 863 331) in 1566, and this attractive building now houses a visitor centre which reveals her story. More recent is **Jedburgh Castle Jail** (ⓣ (01835) 864 750), a model prison built in 1824, with exhibits in the cells and in the former warden's home.

Jedforest Deer and Farm Park (ⓐ Camptown, 8 km/5 miles south of Jedburgh on the A68) offers the chance to see herds of free-roaming red deer and an array of archaic breeds of sheep, cattle, pigs and barnyard fowl.

Jedburgh Tourist Information Office ⓐ Murray's Green ⓣ (0870) 608 0404

Kelso

Like so many of the Border towns, Kelso is now a quiet little market town with little to show for its strategic importance in medieval times – except for the ruins of its abbey. At Smailholm village, **Smailholm Tower** (ⓐ 10 km/6 miles west of Kelso on the A6089/B6937 ⓣ (01573) 460 365) is a stern little relic of the Border

Jedburgh Abbey

Smailholm Tower

wars – a four-sided 15th-century keep surrounded by an outer wall. Within is an exhibition of tapestries that once adorned the walls of local manors and a collection of dolls dressed as characters from Sir Walter Scott's famous *Minstrelsy of the Scottish Border*.

Just outside Kelso, **Floors Castle** (ⓐ Off the A6089 ⓣ (01573) 223 333 ⓦ www.roxburghe.net), the ancestral seat of the local magnates, the Dukes of Roxburghe, is a tower house first extended by William Adam and later remodelled by William Playfair and is grandly decorated and furnished with some superb antiques. **Mellerstain House** (ⓐ Gordon, near Kelso ⓣ (01573) 410 225 ⓦ www.mellerstain.com), also nearby, is a fine Georgian stately home designed by William and Robert Adam, architects of parts of Edinburgh's New Town. The residence of the Earls of Hamilton, it too has splendid interiors.

Kelso Tourist Information Office ⓐ The Square ⓣ (0870) 608 040

Lauder

This small town's main attraction is the nearby **Thirlestane Castle** (ⓐ Thirlestane Castle Trust, Lauder ⓣ (01578) 722 430 ⓦ www.thirlestanecastle.co.uk). Reckoned to be one of the best-preserved castles in Scotland, this red-sandstone fortified manor is everything a romantic stronghold should be, with an array of turrets and battlements. Within, it has lovely decorated ceilings dating from the 17th century, working Victorian kitchens, and an exhibition of historic toys.

Melrose & Galashiels

Melrose, on the banks of the River Tweed, is one of the most striking towns in the Scottish Borders – and one of the oldest. Although the Romans never fully controlled this part of the British Isles, they did build a defensive rampart, Antonine's Wall, between Firth and Clyde in AD 142. Later, they withdrew to the more easily defended line of Hadrian's Wall, but maintained outposts in the region to the north, which they knew as Valentia. Melrose was one of these, and the remains of a legionary fort can be seen beside the Tweed at **Newstead**, about 2 km (1 mile) east of the town centre. The Romans called it Trimontium, after the three Eildon Hills, which overlook Melrose. The circular ramparts of an even older pre-Roman Iron Age fort can be seen on the northernmost of Eildon's triple summits, and there are fine panoramic views from the tall central summit. There are equally fine views of the Eildon summits from **Scott's View**, at

Melrose Abbey

Bemersyde near Melrose, named after Sir Walter Scott. Legend has it that the famous author loved this viewpoint so much that during his funeral the hearse carrying his coffin paused here to allow him a last posthumous glimpse of his beloved Border country.

St Cuthbert's Way, part of a pilgrimage route that in medieval times connected Melrose with the great abbeys of Northumbria, passes between the two tallest peaks of Eildon, and Melrose's fine **abbey** (ⓐ Outskirts of Melrose off the A7 or A68 ⓣ (01896) 822 562), which, though much ruined, is the most evocative sight in town. It was built by Cistercian monks in 1136 and reconstructed in the 14th century. Like the other great religious foundations of the Borders,

ACTIVITIES

Fishing

The River Tweed offers some of the best, most challenging – and most expensive – dry fly-fishing in Scotland, and the best beats are booked at premium prices several years in advance.

Riding

The **British Horse Society** (w www.bhsscotland.org.uk) offers four circular horse-riding trails in the Midlothian area and also offers overnight accommodation for horse and rider.

Rugby

The Borders region is Scotland's rugby heartland. During the rugby season there are matches almost every Saturday in almost every Border town and visitors are welcome. For fixtures, see the **Scottish Rugby Union** website (w www.scottishrugby.org).

Skiing

The Pentland Hills, within sight of Edinburgh, offer year-round skiing even when there is no snow with one of Scotland's longest-established dry ski slopes at Hillend, just outside the city. t (0131) 445 4433

Walking

Walks in the Lothian and Borders area range from gentle countryside ambles to strenuous uphill hiking, many within

the Pentland Hills Regional Park (see page 125), less than 30 minutes from Edinburgh city centre. There is also good walking on the Eildon Hills, near Melrose, and countryside rangers lead a programme of guided walks in the Borders. St Cuthbert's Way, starting at Melrose, is a long-distance walking trail that stretches across the border all the way to the island of Lindisfarne, off the Northumbrian coast.

it suffered from the depredations of English armies and Scottish Protestant reformers, but parts of the graceful nave and choir and much more of its elegant masonry have survived. There's also an interesting museum, with displays of Roman finds from the nearby fort and other relics including a casket containing the heart of Robert the Bruce, exhumed in the 1990s from its last resting place in the abbey gardens. **Dryburgh Abbey** (t (01835) 822 381 w www.historic-scotland.gov.uk 09.30–17.30 daily (Apr–Sept); 09.30–16.30 daily (Oct–Mar)), which dates from about the same period (it was built in 1150) and stands about 8 km (5 miles) south of Melrose, has been much less fortunate, and lies mostly in picturesque ruins except for part of the main abbey church. Sir Walter Scott is buried in the abbey grounds, which stand on the banks of the Tweed and are overshadowed by tall cedars.

Melrose virtually merges with Galashiels, on the west side of the Tweed, although a drab industrial estate lies between the two town centres. Galashiels has a slightly more modern and industrial feel than its neighbour – a hub of the Borders woollen industry for almost five centuries, it has a number of spinning and weaving mills and factory outlet shops. **Abbotsford House** (a 5 km/3 miles

southeast of Galashiels on the A7 (t) (01896) 752 043) was the home of Sir Walter Scott, who had it built in 1822 and stocked it with a collection of memorabilia associated with heroes of his romances of the Lowlands, Highlands and the Border region, including Rob Roy MacGregor's claymore and a flintlock pistol belonging to Viscount Claverhouse of Dundee. Claverhouse was known to his Jacobite friends as Bonnie Dundee, but to his Covenanter enemies as Bloody Claverhouse, for his ruthless suppression of opponents of King James VII and II (of Scotland and England respectively) during the strife of the 1690s, remembered in England as the Glorious Revolution, but in Scotland as the Killing Time.
Melrose Tourist Information Office (a) Next to Melrose Abbey (t) (0870) 608 040

Penicuik

This unassuming village was once the centre of the local lead-mining industry. Lead is a key component in making crystal glass and the region also became a centre for fine glass-making. Edinburgh Crystal ((w) www.edinburgh-crystal.co.uk) is still produced here.

Roslin Glen & Rosslyn Chapel

The amazing, medieval **Rosslyn Chapel** ((a) Roslin (t) (0131) 440 2159 (w) www.rosslynchapel.org.uk), founded in 1446 by Sir William Sinclair, last of the Princes of Orkney, is a remarkable medley of elaborate stone-carving that is surrounded by myths and mysticism. Every inch of masonry within is covered with fantastic symbols and complex decoration, and its history has given rise to dozens of theories involving the vanished Templar crusaders, the Holy Grail and many more mysteries. The famous Apprentice Pillar is the most striking feature, but the chapel also contains many pagan symbols,

Stained-glass window in Rosslyn Chapel

including several Green Men. Most curious of all are carvings that appear to represent plants found only in the Americas made almost half a century before Christopher Columbus sailed to the New World. These are claimed to give credence to the legend that Sir William's ancestor, Prince Henry Sinclair, made a transatlantic voyage of discovery several centuries before Columbus. Nearby, **Roslin Glen Country Park** (ⓐ Off the B7003 between Roslin Village and Rosewell ⓣ (01875) 821 990), beside the North Esk, surrounds the chapel and offers some beautiful country walks through woodland and below steep sandstone cliffs, with the chance to see roe deer, woodpeckers, kestrels and many more birds and animals.

Selkirk

This quiet town was, for many years, the home of the Borders weaving industry. Although its most famous product, the hard-wearing and stylish cloth known to the world as tweed, is commonly associated with the Isle of Harris, its name comes from the river that flows through Selkirk. Sir Walter Scott was the local magistrate for some 30 years, and the 19th-century **Sir Walter Scott's Courtroom** (ⓐ Market Place ⓣ (01750) 20096) is now a museum with portraits of Scott, Robert Burns, and the Selkirk-born Mungo Park, famed for his exploration of West Africa during the 19th century. Nearby, at Innerleithen, **Traquair House** (ⓐ Innerleithen, 2 km (1 mile) off the main A72 road ⓣ (01896) 830 323) is an atmospheric 13th-century keep and mansion with its own brewery, making some of Scotland's finest ales. Philiphaugh, just south of Selkirk, was the scene of a famous defeat for the Royalist cause under the Earl of Montrose at the hands of Cromwell's Parliamentarian troops during the civil wars of the mid-17th century.

RETAIL THERAPY

Gyle Shopping Centre Some say this sizeable complex is the best for shopping in all of the Lothians. A great selection of shops, as well as coffee shops and a food hall, makes this a favourite for all ages. Situated to the west of the city, there are always parking places. ⓐ Gyle Avenue, South Gyle Broadway ⓣ (0131) 539 9000 ⓦ www.gyleshopping.co.uk ⓗ 09.30–20.00 Mon–Wed & Fri, 09.30–21.00 Thur, 09.00–18.00 Sat, 10.00–18.00 Sun

Traquair House Craft Shop This shop sells candles and attractive handmade pottery, and you can also pick up a few bottles of Traquair's famously strong ale. ⓐ Innerleithen ⓣ (01896) 830 323 ⓗ 12.30–17.30 daily (Apr–Oct), closed Nov–Mar

Sir Walter Scott's romantic medieval-style home, Abbotsford

TAKING A BREAK

King's Arms Hotel £ This old-fashioned former coaching inn has been providing pub meals since the 17th century. ⓐ High Street, Melrose ⓣ (01896) 800 335 ⓦ www.kingsarms-melrose.co.uk ⓛ 12.00–14.00, 18.30–21.00 Mon–Fri, 12.00–14.00, 18.30–22.00 Sat, 18.00–21.00 Sun

Monte Cassino £ Unpretentious Italian eating place serving pizza, pasta and salads. ⓐ Old Station Building, Palma Place, Melrose ⓣ (01896) 820 082 ⓛ 12.00–22.00 Mon–Sat, 12.00–20.00 Sun

Marmions Hotel Restaurant ££ Good-value brasserie-style restaurant, long established but does not rest on its laurels. ⓐ 5 Buccleuch Street, Melrose ⓣ (01896) 822 245 ⓛ 11.00–23.00 Mon–Sat, closed Sun

Queen's Bistro ££ Affordable but surprisingly sophisticated bistro serving contemporary and traditional Italian dishes. ⓐ 24 Bridge Street, Kelso ⓣ (01573) 228 899 ⓛ 17.00–24.00 daily

Roxburghe Hotel Restaurant ££ This restaurant has few rivals in the region for fine dining. ⓐ Heiton, Kelso ⓣ (01573) 450 331 ⓛ 10.00–22.00 Mon–Fri, 10.00–23.00 Sat, 10.00–21.00 Sun

ACCOMMODATION

For help with finding somewhere to stay, contact the Edinburgh and Scotland Information Centre (see page 153).

▶ *A tourist bus on the Royal Mile*

PRACTICAL
information

Directory

GETTING THERE

By air

Edinburgh International Airport is serviced by several daily scheduled flights from major British and European cities and there are some 40 flights a day from London to Edinburgh. Please note that UK residents still need to provide photographic ID to check-in with most airlines, usually a passport. Flight time from London is one hour. Low-cost, no-frills airlines such as easyJet, Ryanair and bmibaby also operate flights from the rest of Britain and Europe. There is a daily flight on Continental Airlines between Edinburgh and New York (flight time 7 hours and 40 minutes).

Edinburgh International Airport ⓦ www.edinburghairport.com
bmibaby ⓦ www.bmibaby.com
Continental Airlines ⓦ www.continental.com
easyJet ⓦ www.easyjet.com
Ryanair ⓦ www.ryanair.com

Many people are aware that air travel emits CO_2, which contributes to climate change. You may be interested in the possibility of lessening the environmental impact of your flight through the charity **Climate Care**, which offsets your CO_2 by funding environmental projects around the world. Visit ⓦ www.jpmorganclimatecare.com

By rail

The East Coast rail route from London King's Cross to Edinburgh Waverley passes through Peterborough, Doncaster, York and Newcastle. The journey time is approximately four hours.

East Coast ⓣ (08457) 225 010 ⓦ www.eastcoast.co.uk

By road

National Express coaches make the journey between London and Edinburgh eight times a day, with an average journey time of 11 hours, depending on traffic and time of day (t (08717) 81 81 78 w www.nationalexpress.com).

Edinburgh is easily reached by the M1/A1 route and the M6/M74 motorways from the east and west of Britain respectively. Both the **AA** (w www.theaa.com) and the **RAC** (w www.rac.co.uk) offer route-planning services on their websites to help plan your journey.

Waverley Station in the heart of the city

ENTRY FORMALITIES

Visitors from most European countries do not need a visa to enter Britain (exceptions include Albania, Bosnia, Croatia, Macedonia, Montenegro and Serbia) and can stay for up to three months. Citizens from EU countries need only a valid passport and can stay indefinitely. Visitors from Canada, the United States, Australia and New Zealand do not need a visa and can stay for up to six months, as long as they have adequate funds and a return ticket.

Visitors from within the EU are entitled to bring their personal effects and goods for personal consumption and not for resale, which can be up to 800 cigarettes and 10 litres of spirits. Those entering the country from outside the EU may bring in 200 cigarettes (250 g tobacco, 50 cigars), 2 litres of non-sparkling wine and 1 litre of strong liqueur or 2 litres of sparkling wine or fortified wine, such as sherry or port.

MONEY

The pound (£) is the official currency of Great Britain. £1 = 100 pence. It comes in notes of £5, £10, £20 and £50. Coins are in denominations of £1 and £2 and 1, 2, 5, 10, 20 and 50 pence. One aspect that often confuses visitors to Scotland is that Scottish banknotes come in three different designs, representing the Bank of Scotland, the Royal Bank of Scotland and the Clydesdale Bank. English banknotes are, however, entirely legal tender in Scotland. It might be advisable to change the notes back into English banknotes at the end of your stay. Even in England, where they are also legal tender, many smaller shopkeepers can be confused by them and refuse to take them, and they are extremely difficult to exchange abroad.

ATMs (known as cashpoints) can be found outside banks and many other areas and are open 24 hours a day. The most widely accepted credit cards are VISA and MasterCard, but American Express is also accepted in larger hotels and more expensive restaurants and shops. Traveller's cheques and foreign money can be exchanged at larger banks and at bureaux de change.

HEALTH, SAFETY & CRIME

Visitors to Scotland are unlikely to encounter any food or drink issues – tap water is safe to drink although bottled water is also available everywhere.

Medical facilities are run by the National Health Service (NHS), which entitles British citizens and citizens of the EU to free medical care. Visitors from outside these areas should make sure they have adequate health insurance to avoid having to pay for any medical care should they fall ill. If you take prescriptive drugs, make sure you bring an adequate supply as well as a letter from your doctor or personal health record card. Most minor ailments can be diagnosed and treated at pharmacies throughout the city and, unlike many other countries, mild pain relief, such as aspirin, can often be bought at small grocery shops and in supermarkets, as well as at pharmacies.

Edinburgh has been voted one of the safest cities in Europe, and visitors in the centre are unlikely to feel at risk in any way, although certain areas, such as the backstreets of Leith, should be avoided at night. Any crime should be reported to the police straight away.

For advice on what to do in an emergency, see page 154.

OPENING HOURS

Banks 09.30–16.30 Mon–Fri. Some banks are also open on Saturday mornings. Cash can be obtained 24 hours a day from hole-in-the-wall ATMs.

Pubs, bars & clubs (see page 28)

Shops 09.00–17.30 Mon–Sat. Some shops and department stores open later until 19.00 or 20.00 on Wednesday or Thursday, and have shorter opening hours on Sunday.

TOILETS

Toilet facilities can be found in museums, department stores and shopping centres, and are generally clean and of a high standard. In pubs you would normally be expected to buy a drink before using the facilities, although many landlords and bar staff will kindly overlook this.

CHILDREN

Edinburgh is a child-friendly city and with the smoking ban in place even most pubs will be happy to have children on their premises, although it's always best to check first. All but the poshest restaurants will welcome children, and many offer children's menus. Breastfeeding in pubs and restaurants, however, is generally considered taboo. Many attractions are specifically geared towards children, including Dynamic Earth (see page 62), the Museum of Childhood (see page 74) and the Edinburgh Dungeon (see page 68). Slightly older children will also get a lot out of the National Museum of Scotland (see page 75).

Baby food, nappies and other kiddie paraphernalia can be bought in supermarkets, in high-street chains and at grocery stores.

COMMUNICATIONS

Internet

Internet cafés are dotted all over the city, and you're never likely to be more than a few minutes away from web and email access.

TELEPHONING SCOTLAND

To telephone Edinburgh from abroad, dial 00 44 131 followed by the local number. You do not need to dial the city code (0131) within the city limits.

TELEPHONING ABROAD

To telephone abroad from Scotland, dial 00 followed by the country code, area code (minus the first zero) and local number. Country codes are listed in the phone directory and include: Australia 61, Canada 1, France 33, Germany 49, Ireland 353, New Zealand 64, USA 1.

Phone

The phone numbers given in this book are local numbers, including the Edinburgh area code of (0131).

Public payphones accept either coins or credit cards. Some payphones also offer the option of texting messages. The minimum rate for a cash call is 30p; the minimum rate for a credit-card call is 95p. Unlike much of the rest of the country, the classic red phone box can still be seen everywhere on Edinburgh's city streets.

Post

The British postal service is generally very reliable, with first-class mail arriving at destinations within the UK usually within one day, and in Europe within two or three days (depending on the service at the country of destination). The main post office in the city centre is in the St James Centre (see page 94), which is open all day Monday to Saturday. Most other post offices in the city close at 12.00 or 13.00

on Saturday. Stamps can be bought at post offices, as well as at larger newsagents. Postboxes on the street are the round, red pillar boxes, some of which have separate slots for national and international mail.

First-class stamps within the UK cost 41p, second class 32p. Letters and postcards to Europe weighing up to 20 g cost 60p. To the rest of the world, letters and postcards weighing up to 10 g cost 67p and, up to 20 g, 97p.

Festival-goers on the Royal Mile near St Giles Cathedral

ELECTRICITY

The standard electrical voltage in Britain is 240v with three square-pinned plugs. Foreign appliances will require an adaptor plug, available in your home country, and some US appliances running on 110v may require a transformer.

TRAVELLERS WITH DISABILITIES

Edinburgh is an old city, so cobbled and narrow streets as well as steep hills can prove a challenge for disabled travellers with mobility problems, especially in the Old Town. Many pubs too will prove difficult to access if you are in a wheelchair – even if you are able to enter the establishment, you may not be able to use the toilet facilities. Newer establishments, however, including museums, restaurants and bars, build disabled access into their design by law. **Capability Scotland** (ⓐ 11 Ellersley Road, Edinburgh ⓣ (0131) 337 9876 ⓦ www.capability-scotland.org.uk) provides advice and information about disability issues, while **Tourism For All** (ⓐ Shap Road Industrial Estate, Shap Road, Kendal LA9 6NZ ⓣ (0845) 124 9971 ⓦ www.tourismforall.org.uk) is a national organisation that offers advice about holidays around Britain and transport issues for those with disabilities. **RADAR** (ⓐ 12 City Forum, 250 City Road, London EC1V 8AF ⓣ (020) 7250 3222 ⓦ www.radar.org.uk) offers the same service, as well as advice for other countries.

TOURIST INFORMATION

The city's main tourist office is centrally located on Princes Street and stocks a range of leaflets, literature, guides and maps of the city and the surrounding area, as well as a small selection of souvenirs. Staff are knowledgeable and helpful and can offer advice on attractions, eating out, current events, accommodation, theatre tickets (including

Edinburgh Information Centre on Princes Street

handling bookings), day trips and much more. There's also a very good information centre at Edinburgh Airport.

Edinburgh & Scotland Information Centre ⓐ 3 Princes Street ⓣ (0845) 225 5121 ⓛ 09.00–18.00 daily (Apr & Sept); 09.00–19.00 Mon–Sat, 10.00–19.00 Sun (May & June); 09.00–20.00 daily (July & Aug); 09.00–17.00 Mon–Wed, 09.00–18.00 Thur–Sat, 10.00–17.00 Sun (Oct–Mar)

Airport Information/Tourist Information Desk ⓐ Edinburgh International Airport ⓣ (0870) 040 0007 ⓛ 06.30–22.30 daily (Apr–Oct); 07.00–21.00 daily (Nov–Mar)

The following websites also offer useful information: ⓦ www.edinburgh.org and ⓦ www.visitscotland.com

BACKGROUND READING

Rebus's Scotland by Ian Rankin. The author explores the city through the eyes of his fictional police inspector.

Capital of the Mind: How Edinburgh Changed the World by James Buchan. A history of the Scottish Enlightenment.

Complicity by Iain Banks. Thriller set in various parts of the city.

The Edinburgh Literary Companion by Andrew Lownie. Traces the city's literary past and present.

Regeneration Trilogy by Pat Barker. Novels set partly in Craiglockhart Hospital (now part of Napier University) during World War I.

The Town Below the Ground: Edinburgh's Legendary Underground City by Jan-Andrew Henderson. A history of Edinburgh's tenements, such as that at The Real Mary King's Close (see page 50).

Trainspotting by Irvine Welsh. Modern classic of hard-hitting Leith and its drug problems (see page 105).

Weegies v Edinbuggers by Ian Black. A humorous look at the rivalry between the two Scottish cities.

Emergencies

In an emergency call:
Police ⓣ 999
Ambulance ⓣ 999
Fire Brigade ⓣ 999

Late-night Pharmacy ⓐ Boots, 48 Shandwick Place ⓣ (0131) 225 6757 ⓛ 08.00–21.00 Mon–Sat, 10.00–17.00 Sun. Other late-night pharmacies are listed on the door of any closed pharmacy.

MEDICAL SERVICES

Hospitals

Royal Infirmary of Edinburgh This is the city's main hospital, with a 24-hour accident and emergency department. ⓐ 51 Little France Crescent, Old Dalkeith Road ⓣ (0131) 536 1000
Minor Injury Clinic ⓐ Western General Hospital, Crewe Road South ⓣ (0131) 537 1330 ⓛ 08.00–21.00 daily

Doctors

NHS Direct is a nationwide telephone service that offers professional nursing advice on symptoms and medical conditions. ⓣ (0845) 4647 ⓦ www.nhsdirect.nhs.uk

Dentists

Edinburgh Dental Institute is free but an appointment is necessary. ⓐ Lauriston Building, Lauriston Place ⓣ (0131) 536 4920

POLICE

Police officers can be seen regularly on the streets, dressed in black-and-white uniform and, often, fluorescent yellow jackets. They are friendly and efficient, and can be approached for anything from asking directions to reporting crime. Transport police are on duty at railway stations.

Police HQ ⓐ Fettes Avenue ⓣ (0131) 311 3131 (The most central police station in Edinburgh is on Gayfield Square, near the top of Leith Walk ⓣ (0131) 556 9270.)

EMBASSIES & CONSULATES

Australia ⓐ Mitchell House, 5 Mitchell Street ⓣ (0131) 538 0582
Canada ⓐ 50 Lothian Road, Festival Square ⓣ (0131) 473 6320
New Zealand ⓐ 5 Rutland Square ⓣ (0131) 222 8109
Republic of Ireland ⓐ 16 Randolph Crescent ⓣ (0131) 226 7711
USA ⓐ 3 Regent Terrace ⓣ (0131) 556 8315

The National Monument on Calton Hill is a popular place in summer

ACKNOWLEDGEMENTS

The publishers would like to thank the following for supplying their copyright photographs for this book: BigStockPhoto.com (Rob Cocquyt, page 139; Timothy Large, page 27); Dreamstime.com (David Campbell, pages 108–9; Valeria Cantone, page 150; Philip Dickson, page 57; Domnhall Dods, pages 10–11 & 33; Igor Terekhov, page 80; Ilia Torlin, page 7; Ian Walker, page 29); iStockphoto.com (Jeroen De Mast, pages 44–5; Lisa Fletcher, page 23; StockCube, page 5; TT, page 19); Pictures Colour Library, page 143; The Rocco Forte Collection, page 41; Shutterstock (Chris Jenner, page 107); Stuck on Scotland, pages 12 & 15; SXC.hu (Ove Tøpfer, page 103); Terinea, page 96; Wikimedia Commons (Christian Bickel, page 141); Robin Gauldie, all others.

Project editor: Rosalind Munro
Proofreaders: Karolin Thomas & Jan McCann
Layout: Donna Pedley

Send your thoughts to
books@thomascook.com

- **Found a great bar, club, shop or must-see sight that we don't feature?**
- **Like to tip us off about any information that needs a little updating?**
- **Want to tell us what you love about this handy little guidebook and more importantly how we can make it even handier?**

Then here's your chance to tell all! Send us ideas, discoveries and recommendations today and then look out for your valuable input in the next edition of this title.

Email the above address (stating the title) or write to:
pocket guides Series Editor, Thomas Cook Publishing, PO Box 227, Coningsby Road, Peterborough PE3 8SB, UK.

WHAT'S IN YOUR GUIDEBOOK?

Independent authors Impartial up-to-date information from our travel experts who meticulously source local knowledge.

Experience Thomas Cook's 165 years in the travel industry and guidebook publishing enriches every word with expertise you can trust.

Travel know-how Thomas Cook has thousands of staff working around the globe, all living and breathing travel.

Editors Travel-publishing professionals, pulling everything together to craft a perfect blend of words, pictures, maps and design.

You, the traveller We deliver a practical, no-nonsense approach to information, geared to how you really use it.

Thomas Cook pocket guides
PARIS
Your travelling companion since 1873

Thomas Cook